# Accountability in Public Expenditures in Latin America and the Caribbean

# Accountability in Public Expenditures in Latin America and the Caribbean

*Revitalizing Reforms in Financial Management and Procurement*

Omowunmi Ladipo, Alfonso Sánchez, and Jamil Sopher

**THE WORLD BANK**
**Washington, D.C.**

© 2009 The International Bank for Reconstruction and Development / The World Bank

1818 H Street NW
Washington DC 20433
Telephone: 202-473-1000
Internet: www.worldbank.org
E-mail: feedback@worldbank.org

1 2 3 4 12 11 10 09

This volume is a product of the staff of the International Bank for Reconstruction and Development / The World Bank. The findings, interpretations, and conclusions expressed in this volume do not necessarily reflect the views of the Executive Directors of The World Bank or the governments they represent.

The World Bank does not guarantee the accuracy of the data included in this work. The boundaries, colors, denominations, and other information shown on any map in this work do not imply any judgement on the part of The World Bank concerning the legal status of any territory or the endorsement or acceptance of such boundaries.

**Rights and Permissions**

ISBN: 978-0-8213-7984-4
eISBN: 978-0-8213-7985-1
DOI: 10.1596/978-0-8213-7984-4

Cover photo: *Young Girls with Doctor Hat in Nova Iguaçu* by Achim Pohl, Peter Arnold Inc.

Cover design by Candace Roberts, Quantum Think, Philadelphia, PA, United States

**Library of Congress Cataloging-in-Publication data has been applied for.**

# Contents

**Boxes**

## Tables

# Foreword

Among the most important functions of governments are managing and controlling public resources as well as planning for the future allocation of such resources. The integrity of public financial management and procurement arrangements not only affects the level of trust citizens have in their governments, but also fundamentally determines the connection between policies and impacts on the ground. Transformational leaders realize that a country's competitiveness in the world, its ability to attract foreign investors, and its cost of borrowing are affected by the quality of these core public finance activities.

Central to the achievement of quality public spending are sound public expenditure management arrangements that include: (1) comprehensive and transparent legal frameworks for public financial management and procurement; (2) institutional frameworks made up of agencies with clearly defined responsibilities and adequate numbers of suitably qualified professional staff; (3) leadership that takes seriously its accountability for efficient management of public resources; (4) procurement arrangements that are supportive of governments' strategic goals and that are based on explicit principles of economy, efficiency, competition, and transparency; and (5) independent scrutiny, including from civil society, of governments' stewardship of public resources.

Based on a sample of countries in Latin America and the Caribbean, this book sets out areas in which governments could focus to improve the quality of public expenditures. It seeks to identify, from a regional perspective, first, the cross-cutting strengths and weaknesses of public financial management and procurement systems and, second, the characteristics of and lessons that can be learned from reform programs. In undertaking this analysis, the authors have taken a particular interest in establishing what role civil society organizations may have played, or could play, in promoting transparency and accountability in the public sector.

More specifically, this book focuses on the specific institutional arrangements and the policy choices that underpin the management of public finances, which are set out primarily in a sample of publicly available Country Financial Accountability Assessments and Country Procurement Assessment Reports undertaken by the World Bank and its development partners. The sample is made up of 10 countries (selected to provide a cross section of large and small countries, middle- and low-income countries) for which assessments were undertaken from 2000 to 2005.[1] Where changes since then are considered significant, the book seeks to give a sense of the direction, result, or impact of those changes.

**Roberto Tarallo**
Manager, Financial Management
World Bank
Latin America and the Caribbean
Region

**Enzo De Laurentiis**
Manager, Procurement
World Bank
Latin America and the Caribbean
Region

**Stefan Koeberle**
Director, Strategy and Operations
World Bank
Latin America and the Caribbean
Region

**Charles Griffin**
Senior Fellow
Brookings Institution
Transparency and Accountability
Project

---

1. The 10 countries are Brazil, Chile, Colombia, Costa Rica, Dominican Republic, Guatemala, Honduras, Jamaica, Panama, and Paraguay. Other Country Financial Accountability Assessments and Country Procurement Assessment Reports not included in the sample were also reviewed to confirm the validity of the general conclusions.

# Acknowledgments

This book was made possible through the generous support of the Global Development Program of the Hewlett Foundation and the extensive collaboration of Charles Griffin, senior fellow in the Brookings Institution's Global Economy and Development Program. In addition Chinyere Bun, research associate, Brookings Institution Transparency and Accountability Project, interviewed Bank staff and experts from other organizations and compiled information for the boxes that appear in this volume; and Kyle Peppin, program assistant, Brookings Institution, provided editorial support.

Country Financial Accountability Assessments and Country Procurement Assessment Reports for the World Bank's Latin America and the Caribbean Region are always undertaken in collaboration with the Bank's development partners. Thus, current and past staff from the Inter-American Development Bank provided valuable inputs in the preparation of this book. They were Adriana Arroyave, Roberto Camblor, Sabine Engelhard, Fernando Fernandez, and Deborah Sprietzer.

Others devoted time to reviewing and commenting on this work, and the authors acknowledge their contributions with gratitude. They were Barbara Friday, senior anticorruption adviser, RTI International; Pamela Gomez, formerly project leader, Open Budget Initiative, International Budget Project; Carmen Palladino, former accountant general of

Argentina; Marcela Rozo, senior program coordinator, Public Contracting, Transparency International; and Paul Schapper, former commissioner, State Supply Commission, Government of Western Australia.

Finally, this book would not have been possible without the World Bank staff members who contributed their country perspectives in finalizing the report or fulfilled the role of peer reviewer. They were Alexandre Arrobio, Asha Ayoung, Ana Bellver, Paul Bermingham, Diomedes Berroa, Regis Cunningham, Henri Fortín, Linn Hammergren, Anthony Hegarty, John Hegarty, Els Hinderdael, Patricia De la Fuente Hoyes, Paul Levy, Andres MacGaul, Joao da Veiga Malta, Nicholas Manning, Patricia Mcgowan, Patricia McKenzie, Snezana Mitrovic, Moustapha Ndiaye, Emmanuel Njomo, Alexandre Borges de Oliveira, Melissa Paredes, Chris Parel, James Parks, Maria Poli, Felix Prieto, Maritza Rodriguez, Catherine Rojas, Felipe Saez, Nicola Smithers, Rajeev Swami, Catalina Michelle Tejada, and Luis Tineo.

# About the Authors

**Omowunmi Ladipo** is a fellow of the Institute of Chartered Accountants in England and Wales. Prior to joining the World Bank in 1998, she was an audit partner in a national accounting practice in the United Kingdom. Since joining the Bank, she has worked on public financial management and accountability issues in Bangladesh, Brazil, Cambodia, India, Laos, Malaysia, Mexico, Nepal, Republic of Korea, and Vietnam. She has also served as cochair of the Organisation for Economic Co-operation and Development (OECD) Joint Venture on Public Financial Management and represented the Bank on the Public Expenditure and Financial Accountability (PEFA) Steering Committee. In her current role as the governance and anticorruption coordinator for the World Bank's Latin America and the Caribbean Region, one of her areas of interest is the role that supreme audit institutions (SAI's) and legislatures can play in enhancing accountability and transparency in the management of public finances in the process contributing to good governance.

**Alfonso Sánchez** is an international expert in public contracting and dispute resolution. He has been a consultant in these fields for the World Bank, the Inter-American Development Bank, the OECD, the Canadian International Development Agency, the United Nations, the Brookings Institution, and the Agency for International Cooperation of Japan. He held technical and senior managerial positions at the World Bank in the infrastructure sector for many years and was Director of the Procurement Policy and Services Department and ombudsman of the Bank. Before joining the Bank, he held senior executive positions in the public and private infrastructure sectors in Colombia. Alfonso holds degrees in civil engineering from the National University of Colombia, in natural resources management from the University of Michigan in the United States, and in arbitration from the University of Reading (College of Estate Management) in the United Kingdom.

**Jamil Sopher** is an international financial analyst with 40 years of experience assessing the financial performance of private companies as well as public sector enterprises across Asia, Europe, Latin America, and the United States. Over the past 30 years, he has been affiliated with the World Bank, first as a staff member and later as a consultant. As a staff member, he led lending activities to electricity, water supply and sanitation, telecommunications and transportation utilities, as well as to refineries and development banks. Prior to his retirement, Jamil served as chairman of the World Bank Group's Staff Association. Over the past seven years, he has served as a consultant to the Financial Management Unit for the Latin America and the Caribbean Region, where he provided guidance for assessments of the public financial management systems and practices of about 15 of the region's countries. Jamil holds a Bachelor of Science and a Master of Engineering (Electrical) from Cornell University and a Master of Business Administration from Harvard University.

# Acronyms

| | |
|---|---|
| ADR | alternative dispute resolution |
| CFAA | Country Financial Accountability Assessment |
| CPA | Certified Public Accountant |
| CPAR | Country Procurement Assessment Report |
| CSO | civil society organization |
| EU | European Union |
| FASB | Financial Accounting Standards Board |
| FDI | foreign direct investment |
| FTA | free trade agreement |
| GAAP | Generally Accepted Accounting Principles |
| GATT | General Agreement on Trade and Tariffs |
| GDP | gross domestic product |
| GFS | government finance statistics |
| GPA | Government Procurement Agreement |
| HIPC | heavily indebted poor country |
| IAS | International Accounting Standards |
| IASB | International Accounting Standards Board |
| IASC | International Accounting Standards Committee |
| IFAC | International Federation of Accountants |
| IFRS | International Financial Reporting Standards |

| IMF | International Monetary Fund |
|-----|-----|
| INTOSAI | International Organization of Supreme Audit Institutions |
| IPSAS | International Public Sector Accounting Standard |
| IPSASB | International Public Sector Accounting Standards Board |
| LAC | Latin America and the Caribbean |
| OECD | Organisation for Economic Co-operation and Development |
| PEFA | Public Expenditure and Financial Accountability (Initiative) |
| PEM | public expenditure management |
| PFM | public financial management |
| ROSC (A&A) | Report on the Observance of Standards and Codes (Accounting & Auditing) |
| SAI | supreme audit institution |
| TI | Transparency International |
| UNCITRAL | United Nations Commission on International Trade Law |
| UNDP | United Nations Development Programme |
| US GAAP | U.S. Generally Accepted Accounting Principles |
| WTO | World Trade Organization |

# What Are Country Financial Accountability Assessments and Country Procurement Assessment Reports?

This book looks at the specific institutional arrangements and the policy choices that underpin the management of public finances in the Latin American and Caribbean region. It draws primarily from a sample of publicly available Country Financial Accountability Assessments and Country Procurement Assessment Reports undertaken at regular intervals by the World Bank and its development partners.

Until 2004 both CFAAs and CPARs were part of a suite of core diagnostic instruments that were maintained and updated for all countries with which the World Bank was engaged.[1] Since then, public financial management diagnostics have been driven by country-specific circumstances and requirements—that is, their nature and scope are based on the type and level of Bank engagement, country priorities, and the availability of information from other development institutions and the country itself.

---

1. Assessments were undertaken at least every five years. As a result, up-to-date CFAAs and CPARs undertaken by the Bank or jointly with its development partners are available for almost all Latin American and Caribbean countries with active World Bank portfolios.

## Country Financial Accountability Assessments

A Country Financial Accountability Assessment (CFAA) supports a country's development objectives by identifying strengths and weaknesses in its public financial management systems. The CFAA facilitates a common understanding between governments and their development partners of how well the institutions responsible for managing the country's public finances are performing. This common understanding helps both governments and their partners identify priorities for action and informs the design and implementation of reform programs. The CFAA is designed to assess the entire budget cycle, including: budget formulation and execution; accounting and reporting; cash, debt, and revenue management; treasury operations; internal controls and audit; external audit; and legislative oversight.

## Country Procurement Assessment Reports

A Country Procurement Assessment Report (CPAR) diagnoses the robustness of a country's procurement system and, in the process, facilitates dialogue with the government on needed reforms. To this end, its primary objectives are to:

- Provide a comprehensive analysis of a country's public sector procurement system, including its legal frameworks, organizational responsibilities, control and oversight capabilities, procedures and practices, and how well these work in practice;
- Undertake a general assessment of the institutional, organizational, and other risks associated with the procurement process, including identifying procurement practices unacceptable for use in Bank-financed projects;
- Develop a prioritized action plan to bring about institutional improvements;
- Assess the competitiveness and performance of the private sector in its participation in public procurement and the adequacy of commercial practices that relate to public procurement.

Specifically, public financial management analytic work is now expected to facilitate and encourage country leadership in setting and managing a public financial management reform strategy within a multiyear framework of sequenced priorities.

In recent years, the World Bank has participated in and served as secretariat for the Public Expenditure and Financial Accountability

(PEFA) Initiative, a partnership of multilateral and bilateral development agencies that have worked together to harmonize the public financial management approaches of development institutions. This participation has culminated in the issuance of a public financial management performance measurement framework, which is intended to serve as an integrated, harmonized approach to measuring and monitoring public financial management performance progress as well as a tool for focusing support on country-led public financial management reform programs. The framework draws on international standards and incorporates a set of high-level indicators that cover the entire budget cycle and a public financial management performance report that enables the indicators to be read and understood in context. In 2005 the PEFA framework replaced the Country Financial Accountability Assessment as the principal tool for assessing country public financial management performance.

Meanwhile, the international interest in government procurement has been growing, triggering both a transformation of public procurement into a strategic government function that supports policy implementation and a better understanding of the importance of national procurement systems that meet internationally recognized good practices. Since 2005 the Organisation for Economic Co-operation and Development (OECD) through its Joint Venture on Procurement (a subcommittee of the OECD Working Party on Aid Effectiveness) has been developing a methodology for the assessment of national procurement systems. This tool, which, it is hoped, will be universally recognized, can be used to assess the quality and effectiveness of national procurement systems with the expectation that countries will improve their systems to meet internationally recognized standards. Although the OECD/DAC (Development Assistance Committee) Methodology for Assessment of National Procurement Systems is still being tested, the World Bank has adopted many of its performance indicators in undertaking procurement diagnostic work.

# CHAPTER 1

# Overview

The Latin America and Caribbean (LAC) region, comprising over 30 countries, is a highly diverse mix of large and small countries; populations and influences—indigenous, Spanish, Portuguese, British, French, and Dutch; and significant disparities in wealth, ranging from a gross domestic product (GDP) per capita of $1,090 in Haiti to $22,183 in Trinidad and Tobago (World Development Indicators Database 2007 data).[1] At the same time, these countries have important commonalities. Poverty remains widespread—for example, the poverty rate is 17.6 percent in Mexico and 64.6 percent in Bolivia (World Bank 2008d).[2] Countries in the region have experienced relatively slow growth—average growth rates lagged those in East Asia through most of the 1990s (3.07 percent compared with 8.79 percent). And many countries, even before the onset of the ongoing global financial crises, suffered from high debt-to-GDP ratios, which in 2007 were, for example, 45.07 percent in Brazil, 127.5 percent in Jamaica, 52.8 percent in Panama, and 46.6 percent in Costa Rica.[3]

Because of these high levels of debt burden, it is not surprising that, after deducting government salaries and pensions, debt service, and pre-allocated or earmarked expenditures, the LAC countries have limited fiscal space to undertake public sector investment programs that underpin growth, reduce poverty, and provide a basic level of services to their populations. Faced with this situation, the LAC governments must continue to focus on reforms in the management of public finances to make those finances more transparent and accountable and to facilitate the efficient and effective delivery of services. In the process, these governments will obtain legitimacy for their stewardship.[4]

In view of the current global financial crises, which began in 2007, the need to maintain momentum in public financial management (PFM) reforms, particularly those leading to greater efficiency and transparency, is even more critical on four fronts.

First, the plunge in commodity prices of 69 percent and oil prices of 46 percent during the last quarter of 2008 and the dramatic slowdown in world trade have had an impact on the "real" economies of the LAC countries.[5] Government revenues are coming under even more pressure at the same time that higher unemployment is exerting upward pressure on the expenditure front. Greater efficiency in government spending will therefore be the order of the day for some time to come.

Second, it is now anticipated that foreign direct investment (FDI) to emerging countries will fall to about $165 billion in 2009 from $466 billion in 2008 and $929 billion in 2007 (IIF 2009). Emerging countries, many in the LAC region, are likely to bear the brunt of this decline. Because of the origins of the financial crises, the emerging market countries with the most robust and transparent financial management arrangements that meet internationally accepted standards will be among the first countries to benefit from the resumed volumes of FDI.

Third, governments across the region, like many governments elsewhere, are adopting a range of fiscal policy measures, including stimulus-type packages, in an attempt to mitigate the worst effects of the global financial crises.[6] By promulgating unprecedented transparency arrangements for its own stimulus plan, the United States has set a precedent that civil society across the world, and particularly in the neighboring LAC region, is likely to demand.[7]

Finally, a new global regulatory architecture is in the cards. This reform, too, will likely imply that LAC countries will have to step up from reliance on national standards to compliance with international standards and benchmarks of performance in accounting, procurement, auditing, and reporting in order for national banks, financial institutions, and private sector corporations to compete in a recrafted global financial architecture. Governments in the region will need to accelerate progress in attaining investment-grade ratings for their sovereign debt, both to reduce costs and to encourage investment.

With the emergence of an increasingly assertive middle class throughout the region, it is also clear that the internal demand for improved accountability, transparency, and performance by governments will grow. Although trust in government has increased (from 19 percent in 2003 to 44 percent in 2008), only about 20 percent of the public believes public institutions are doing a very good or good job, and 70 percent still believes that governments exist to protect the interests of a few. It is perhaps not surprising that citizens of the LAC region are more tolerant of tax evasion (2.2 in 1998 versus 3.5 in 2008 on a scale of 1 to 10), or that they see greater accountability as a prerequisite in order to trust their governments. When asked to rate the most important factors that determine trust in public institutions, respondents in a survey rated audits second only to equality of access. And there has been a significant increase—from 49 percent in 2001 to 57 percent in 2008—in those who acknowledge that the legislature has a legitimate role to play in democracies, perhaps recognizing the role that such a body has to play in strengthening overall accountability arrangements.[8]

This book sets out, based on a sample of LAC countries, areas in which governments should concentrate to improve the quality of public expenditures (see box 1.1). Although the budget process encompasses four

---

**Box 1.1**

## Peru: The Impact of Efficient and Competitive Procurement

A 2008 World Bank report, *Social Safety Nets in Peru*, recommended that Peru concentrate on improving accountability mechanisms to generate better development outcomes from its largest social programs (World Bank 2008c). In particular, the report identified weaknesses arising from the procurement strategy employed by the biggest food program, the municipally administered Vaso de Leche. Vaso de Leche's budget of about S/. 363 million a year accounts for almost half of all of Peru's spending on food programs. The program reaches almost 3 million people (11 percent of the population) with benefits worth on average about S/. 10 ($3) per person per month.

The report identified two factors related to procurement strategy that make the program's costs higher than necessary: uncompetitive procurement and suboptimal specification of the nutritional content of the program's rations.

*(continued)*

**Box 1.1** *(Continued)*

In the area of competition, the report found that in the 14 municipalities visited for the study the procurement processes used were overwhelmingly uncompetitive. Seventy-five percent of the processes evaluated were for small values or for sole-source purchases. Furthermore, many municipalities use sole-source contracting and expedited procedures to sidestep the complexity of Peru's competitive procurement rules. Of the 108 processes reviewed, only 30 used competitive bidding processes, and 12 of those became embroiled in contract award disputes (impugnación).

The most obvious reason for resorting to uncompetitive processes is that they are faster. Public bidding processes average 47 days and may stretch up to 90 days. When there is an impugnación, it averages 76 days and can go on for up to 124 days. By contrast, direct adjudications take between 20 and 30 days on average, and renewals of existing contracts are instantaneous.

The reforms suggested by the study could, if implemented, result in savings estimated at up to S/. 150 million, or over 40 percent of the program's budget and more than enough to offset the impact of the recent inflation in food prices.

stages—preparation, approval, execution, and audit/evaluation—this book focuses primarily on budget execution and audit/evaluation processes. It seeks to identify from a regional perspective cross-cutting strengths and weaknesses in public financial management and procurement arrangements, and the characteristics of and lessons that can be learned from various reform programs. Although the authors acknowledge the importance of underlying civil service arrangements to quality public expenditure management, this book, while pointing out areas in which civil service arrangements merit greater scrutiny, looks largely at the outcomes and impacts of existing public financial management arrangements.

This book focuses on the specific institutional arrangements and the policy choices that underpin the management of public finances in a sample of publicly available Country Financial Accountability Assessments (CFAAs) and Country Procurement Assessment Reports (CPARs) undertaken by the World Bank and its development partners (see earlier box on these tools). The sample consists of 10 countries (selected to provide a cross section of large and small countries, middle- and low-income countries) for which assessments were undertaken from 2000 to 2005. The 10 countries are Brazil, Chile, Colombia, Costa Rica, Dominican Republic, Guatemala, Honduras, Jamaica, Panama, and Paraguay. In addition, this book draws on information from other LAC countries (Argentina, Guyana, Mexico, and Peru) where the related CFAAs and CPARs provide additional insights about the general conclusions.

Public financial management arrangements comprise (1) comprehensive and transparent legal and institutional frameworks embodied in the budget process and made up of agencies with clearly defined responsibilities and adequate numbers of suitably qualified professional staff; (2) leadership that takes seriously its accountability for efficient management of public resources; (3) procurement arrangements that are supportive of governments' strategic goals and based on explicit principles of economy, efficiency, competition, and transparency; and (4) independent scrutiny of governments' stewardship of public resources. Over time, multiple global developments have contributed to internationally recognized benchmarks of performance in each of these areas. Some of the more important of these developments have been:

- Maturation and expansion of the European Union (EU) under which the harmonization of laws, implementing regulations, and practices for financial management and procurement across countries has been a primary concern;
- Technological advances beginning in the early 1990s that made available new tools that revolutionized the ways in which governments could do business;
- Founding of Transparency International (TI) in 1993 and its focus on corruption in the management of public finances;
- Development of codes of good practices and standards such as the Cadbury Code (U.K.), COSO (Committee of Sponsoring Organizations) Framework (U.S.), and the Sarbanes-Oxley Act of 2002 (U.S.);
- Establishment of the World Trade Organization (WTO) in 1995;
- Issuance in November 1997 of the OECD Convention on Combating Bribery of Foreign Public Officials in International Business Transactions;
- Coming of age of internationally recognized bodies that issue international accounting, financial reporting, and auditing standards that establish a level playing field in both the private and public sectors;
- Establishment in 2001 of the Public Expenditure and Financial Accountability Initiative, followed by the issuance in 2005 of a public financial management performance measurement framework[9];
- Recognition of the need for international benchmarks of performance in public procurement and the commencement of work, sponsored by the OECD, on defining them.

Globally, internationally recognized standards and benchmarks are now available in budgeting, accounting, reporting and auditing, corporate governance, and sovereign credit ratings. It is against these standards that this book seeks to identify reforms on which LAC governments should focus as they seek to improve their management of public finances over the next decade.

## Public Financial Management Context in the Region

PFM arrangements in the LAC region are heavily influenced by a unique confluence of colonial legal heritage (Napoleonic or Roman law in which rules are codified and prescriptive, and procedural formalities are traditionally observed strictly) and an extreme fragmentation of parties in legislatures.[10] The result is cumbersome, formalistic legislation that often fails to incorporate international good practices or to support the country's economic development policies and objectives. At the same time, PFM systems remain premised on a traditional compliance and control approach, with less focus on issues of efficiency, performance, and value for money.

More specifically, accounting largely remains a bookkeeping function performed by practitioners who learned their trade in high school or university, following nonstandardized curricula. Few countries rely on a special exam for entry into the profession, and although some countries acknowledge the need to refresh practitioners' skills, the availability of continuing professional education is limited. This situation stands in contrast to the practice in most OECD countries, where accounting is a professional function, with standardized entrance exams, and practitioners are required to undergo a specified minimum number of hours of continuing professional education.

Auditing in the region is still largely viewed as a compliance function, premised on ex ante controls over financial transactions. The main qualification for becoming an auditor is previous practice as an accountant for a number of years. The profession is again different in OECD countries, where a structured approach to attaining and maintaining an audit qualification is prevalent, and the emphasis is increasingly on efficient and effective management.

In the area of procurement, because of the prevailing control orientation, preparation of laws and other legal norms has traditionally been left almost exclusively to the legal experts, with a bias toward process and legality. Policymakers continue to see procurement as an administrative process and not as an important economic activity that supports development and promotes attainment of a government's strategic goals. Thus there has been little input from procurement experts, policymakers, or public sector economists, who could advocate for economic efficiency or commercial practice as alternatives around which laws should be drafted. In addition, the triggers for reforms have often been scandals, major corruption cases, or accumulated frustration with the system. In these circumstances, reforms have generally been carried out hastily by adding more controls and passing legislation to deal with crises, but without a thorough analysis of the roots of the problem. Thus with few exceptions, reforms have not been the subject of careful planning, political consensus, and competent management.

Additionally, business groups have become an important driver in shaping the present regulatory framework for procurement in the region. Professional and trade associations have pressed for reforms on two fronts, one positive and one less so. On one front, they have lobbied for simplification of the bidding processes to reduce transaction costs. On the other, they have promoted protectionist legislation—for example, through excluding foreign firms from national bidding or by granting excessive and unjustified price preferences or other special treatment to domestic firms. The result is that progress has been limited in streamlining the regulatory framework, while protection of local firms has increased, arguably stifling competition and impeding the development of local industry into world-class companies that can compete in global markets.

Finally, the predominance of procedural formalities over sound business practices in procurement has resulted in the development of a culture of risk aversion and excessive rigor in the application of norms that continues to affect the willingness of firms to compete for business with the government. It is simply too costly, in many cases, for them to do so.

Some perspective on the standing of the LAC region's PFM performance in the global context can be gained by looking at data on the number of countries that have attained investment-grade ratings for their sovereign debt, because award of these ratings is based in part on the soundness of a country's public finances. As of mid-2008, 87 countries worldwide had attained investment-grade ratings from Moody's. These countries include all those that recently acceded to the EU, the major emerging market countries, and most of the newly industrialized countries of East Asia. In the LAC region, only Brazil, Chile, Costa Rica, El Salvador, Mexico, Panama, Peru, and St. Vincent and the Grenadines have achieved investment-grade ratings.

## Main Findings

Fiscal discipline and public sector efficiency became prominent issues in the Latin America context in the late 1980s. From 1973 to 1987, Latin America's external debt increased by about $349 billion, while capital flight from the region amounted to about $151 billion (Pastor 1990). Meanwhile, the region's GDP grew an average of only about 2 percent from 1980 to 2002 (Ocampo 2003: 3). In the late 1980s, U.S. Treasury Secretary Nicholas Brady proposed a program of debt relief for the region predicated on adopting policies aimed at reducing capital flight. This approach implied containing inflation, implementing effective tax policies, committing to fiscal discipline, and taking steps to improve the overall efficiency and effectiveness of the public sector.

Countries across the region thus embarked on a first wave of reforms that largely focused on updating legal and regulatory frameworks or improving management information systems. However, progress has been uneven both across countries and in implementation of the individual reform programs.

Overall, the 10 countries sampled can be divided into three categories of performance: those making good progress, those making some progress, and those in which there has been little progress. In the first category are Chile and Brazil. Both have made a clear commitment to achieving fiscal discipline and allocating resources strategically. Both countries also are in the process of overcoming legacies of state capture, and they are making, or have made, the institutional and cultural changes needed to underpin sustainability. In the second category are Costa Rica and Panama, but their reliance on off- budget activities has impeded the alignment between available resources and articulated commitments to policies and programs and their reliance on ex ante controls has impeded a results focus. The remaining countries fall into the third category. In these countries, the progress to date is still largely focused on introducing automated PFM systems.

From the sample of countries reviewed, it is clear that, on the one hand, the greatest strides have been made in:

- Automating information systems;
- Establishing budgets that are generally comprehensive;
- Achieving aggregate fiscal discipline.

On the other hand, significant challenges remain in dealing with the:

- Proliferation of procurement regulations and procedures;
- Lack of a professional procurement cadre;

- Availability of budget execution information;
- Focus on transaction-specific ex ante reviews instead of on ex post performance monitoring (internal control frameworks and internal audits);
- Weak nonexecutive independent oversight arrangements (external audits, civil society, and legislative oversight);
- Mismatch between the extent of fiscal decentralization and the limited subnational administrative capacity.

Each of these areas is examined in turn in the sections that follow.

### Automated Information Systems

A necessary, though not sufficient, requirement for governments to be able to make appropriate decisions is that data and information on budget execution expenditures be available on a timely, accurate, and accessible basis. Today, meeting this requirement entails a high degree of automation. Virtually all of the budget and accounting systems in use among the countries reviewed were found to be capable of providing adequate information. Some of the newer systems are able to provide information beyond the purely financial to also include monitoring and evaluation indicators, at least at the national level. Even though some countries had aging infrastructure that needed updating (Brazil, Chile), every country reviewed had a computerized accounting system, and most were integrated with the budget system.

The progress in developing electronic procurement platforms was also encouraging. Most countries now see e-procurement as an essential component of modernization and greater transparency and efficiency. Brazil, Chile, and Mexico pioneered the use of e-procurement. Colombia, Panama, and Paraguay have completed a first phase of system enhancements that provide information on business opportunities and regulations, and they are launching a second phase to establish transactional capabilities with links to budget execution systems.

Some of the important remaining challenges in this area are consolidating information from subnational activities (Chile alone did so to a limited extent); fully integrating financial management systems to include treasury single accounts, procurement planning, and contract monitoring (Dominican Republic, Jamaica); unifying capital and recurrent budgets; and better integrating procurement with budget planning systems and procurement implementation with budget execution.

### Budget Comprehensiveness

An annual budget should provide a comprehensive view of fiscal fore-casts, budget proposals, and previous year out-turns so that it can be subjected to an informed review by the legislative branch of government. Most countries in the LAC region had comprehensive budget systems at the central government level; autonomous agencies were included on a net (or summarized) basis. Important exceptions, however, were found in Argentina, Chile (which uses profits from its national copper company to finance the activities of its Ministry of Defense, and yet neither entity was included in the budget), Costa Rica, Guatemala, and Paraguay.

### Aggregate Fiscal Discipline

As described earlier, a legacy of repeated debt crises across the region resulted in an early and concerted focus on achieving aggregate fiscal discipline—that is, the notion that government spending should be closely aligned with what is affordable over the medium term and, in turn, with the annual budget. As a result of this focus, fiscal responsibility laws, or their equivalent, are in place in Brazil, Chile, Colombia, and Panama, and most other governments are now committed to operating within a balanced budget framework.

### A Proliferation of Procurement Regulations and Procedures

The prevailing institutional model for administering procurement is one of centralized legislation and decentralized management of procurement by individual government agencies and ministries. Regulation generally consists of a national procurement law (in some countries separate laws are in place for goods, civil works, and services) and one or more associated regulatory decrees. Detailed regulations and procedures are generally left to each agency. In addition, in countries with federal arrangements (such as Argentina, Brazil, and Mexico) the states or provinces have their own laws and regulations. This multiplicity of procurement regimes and the diversity of detailed regulations at the agency level have a direct impact on costs and result in market segmentation or reduced competition because suppliers tend to specialize in bidding for contracts with one or a few government agencies. Another consequence is that a "club mentality" develops and often leads to collusion and other abuses. For example, in Costa Rica contractors indicated that it is easier for them to specialize in bidding for work at a single or a few agencies where they know the rules so well.

In an effort to mitigate the impact of this proliferation of regulations and procedures, several countries have created organizations or units to oversee the performance of procurement operations, undertake analytical work on markets and develop supply strategies, issue regulations and procedures, formulate policies, provide training, and resolve precontractual disputes, among other things. However, most of these agencies do not have the resources or the political support to perform their duties, and so they struggle to fulfill their mandates.

This proliferation of regulations is a formidable barrier to the adoption of internationally recognized good practices of access and equal treatment and also complicates the negotiation of free trade agreements (FTAs) in which procurement harmonization is invariably an important item on the agenda. The existence of multiple regulatory regimes also increases the legal risks for those doing business with the government—a particularly critical issue in a region traditionally averse to arbitration or other forms of alternative dispute resolution.[11] Court practices and proceedings, even for relatively simple disputes, are widely considered to be unreliable, unpredictable, costly, and slow, a situation that worsens when disputes are settled by provincial or state courts in federal regimes. Bidders therefore factor this risk into their prices or are discouraged from participating.

### *Professionalization of Procurement Staff*

The present public procurement function requires well-trained professionals who are capable of working in complex and sophisticated business environments. In the LAC region, however, the procurement function has traditionally been weaker than other public service functions, and agency managers continue to place little strategic value on it. As a result, in all the countries reviewed the lack of a professional cadre of procurement staff was found to be a critical issue hindering effective and efficient procurement operations. In particular:

- Turnover of staff, particularly those in managerial positions, is frequent; it arises from changes in administration and from political interference;
- There is no procurement career stream. Selection and promotion are rarely competitive or merit-based; instead, they tend to be based on political, social, or professional connections;
- In general, the heads of procurement units and their staff do not have the expertise or the formal training required to perform the function.

Learning is undertaken on the job, perpetuating the vices and practices of the past.

### Budget Execution Reporting

As discussed earlier, automated information systems are a prerequisite for informed government decision making on appropriate spending. Another requirement is that information be produced in a form that enables governments to monitor the actual performance of programs. However, significant capacity constraints remain. Specifically, information systems that include the following features are essential, but they are still not widespread:

- *Budget classification.* Budgets should be compiled using a system of expenditure classifications that enable budget staff to monitor resources allocated for specific purposes—that is, program classification. Only Brazil, Chile, Costa Rica, and Panama use programmatic budgetary classifications. Typically, administrative classification systems (resources allocated at the agency level) remain the norm, for example, in Colombia, Dominican Republic, Guatemala, Honduras, Jamaica, and Paraguay. Governments are thus unable to determine whether priority programs received the intended levels of funding unless each program is managed entirely within a single agency.

- *Recurrent and capital budgets.* Budgets should integrate the resource requirements for recurrent costs and capital investments to ensure that that the impact of investments on recurrent costs is fully understood. Only Brazil, Chile, and Costa Rica integrate their investment and recurrent budgets.

- *Chart of accounts.* Budget classifications should be embedded within the chart of accounts, because it is easier to ensure that allocations are spent as intended when both systems are fully aligned or integrated.[12] Costa Rica and Panama were the only two countries that had budget and accounting systems that were fully aligned and integrated. Brazil, Chile, Guatemala, Honduras, and Paraguay had budget and accounting systems that were aligned, but the systems were not integrated, and the remaining countries' systems were neither aligned nor integrated.

- *Subnational reporting.* National governments should be able to monitor the actual use of resources in subnational agencies. In the larger federal countries (Argentina, Brazil, Mexico), a significant proportion of subnational budgets are funded through per capita or constitutionally mandated fiscal transfers. Such transfers are typically included in the national government's budget, but, with the exception of Chile, subnational budget execution information was usually not included in the national government's budget.

The cumulative effect of these budget execution reporting weaknesses is that it is difficult to track how budget allocations are actually spent and even more difficult to verify that the funds are spent for the purpose intended.

### *Internal Control and Internal Audit*

The modern concept of an internal control framework is that it should provide assurance that the objectives associated with the reporting, effectiveness and efficiency of operations, and compliance with applicable laws and regulations, can be attained. Internal audit is part of this internal control framework. With the exception of Chile and to a lesser extent Costa Rica, the development of formal internal control frameworks that are aligned with internationally recognized standards is still in its infancy. A common feature in the countries reviewed is that governments tend to rigorously apply ex ante transaction-specific reviews that serve to confirm legality and regularity, but that by their nature are time-intensive and reduce operational efficiency. Rarely considered is the risk environment: the personal and professional integrity and ethical values of the executive and civil servants; a commitment to competence; the executive's philosophy and operating style (i.e., the "tone at the top"); the organizational structure, including a measure of independence for the internal audit function; and human resource policies and practices—all of which are prerequisites for a sound control environment.

The underlying causes of weakness in these areas differed across the countries reviewed. They include shortages of suitably qualified staff (Brazil, Dominican Republic, Guatemala, Honduras, Jamaica, Paraguay); insufficient budgetary resources (Colombia, Guatemala); lack of quality control (Colombia, Costa Rica, Paraguay); lack of appreciation for this function among public sector managers; and lack of authority to follow up and correct deficiencies identified by internal audits.

The key impact of weak capacity in these areas is that any effort to increase the efficiency and effectiveness of government programs is rarely influenced by what, in international best practice, is a built-in loop-back mechanism to inform government decisions on where changes should be made.

### External Audit

The external audit function is "an indispensable part of a regulatory system whose aim is to reveal deviations from accepted standards and violations of the principles of legality, efficiency, effectiveness and economy of financial management early enough to make it possible to take corrective action in individual cases, to make those accountable accept responsibility, to obtain compensation, or to take steps to prevent—or at least render more difficult—such breaches" (INTOSAI 1977). The external audit function in the countries reviewed is generally more effective than the internal audit function, and their supreme audit institutions (SAIs) are broadly independent. In most countries, the supreme auditor is appointed by the legislature or a specially constituted legislative committee. Prima facie, the independence test is thus largely met. Important issues that still must be addressed in this area include:

- *Prohibiting SAIs from undertaking executive functions.* This prohibition is needed to minimize the potential for impaired objectivity. Examples are SAI involvement in designing and implementing ex ante controls (Costa Rica, Panama); SAI possession of regulatory authority for specifying the accounting principles applicable to the public sector (Chile, Colombia); SAI participation in ex ante and concurrent review amounting to co-management of the procurement process (Chile, Costa Rica, Panama); and SAI responsibility for preparing the country's annual accounts (Chile).

- *Substantially enhancing the requirement for continuing professional development* across most of the countries, including Brazil, Costa Rica, Dominican Republic, Honduras, Jamaica, and Paraguay.

- *Introducing risk and performance-based auditing* so that SAIs not only focus their audits on the legality and regularity of financial transactions, but also have the space to engage in performance auditing oriented toward examining the performance, economy, efficiency, and effectiveness of public financial management.

- *Applying the appropriate sanctions* in response to negative audit findings on a timely basis. None of the SAIs in the countries reviewed had the authority to apply sanctions to address identified deficiencies, although both Brazil and Chile have a record of agencies responding to audit findings. In some countries (Dominican Republic, Paraguay), the SAI does not have authority to follow up its findings, whereas in others (Guatemala, Jamaica) the SAIs lack an enforcement mechanism.

- *Providing the legal mandate and the capacity* so that SAIs audit all public operations regardless of whether or how they are reflected in the national accounts. As noted earlier, some countries in the sample use off-budget entities or other nontransparent budgetary mechanisms. Chile ensures that such agencies are audited and makes public summary financial information about those agencies. In Brazil, the SAI has the responsibility to audit all 1,100 government agencies. However, it lacks the staff to fulfill this obligation. In other countries (Dominican Republic, Guatemala, Honduras, Paraguay), the SAIs are permitted to audit state-owned enterprises and other off-budget agencies, but they lack the capacity to fulfill that responsibility.

These deficiencies result in external audit functions that are neither timely nor robust enough to influence the efficiency or effectiveness of government operations. Only in rare cases (Chile, Panama) do public sector managers use information obtained from the external audit to identify and address operational weaknesses.

### Civil Society

There is increasing recognition that civil society participation and oversight are key elements of any balanced system of accountability—that is, more governments now acknowledge that civil society participation lends them legitimacy and credibility. Unfortunately, the weaker the system, the less involved the civil society organizations (CSOs) seemed likely to be. For example, in the Dominican Republic where PFM systems were generally weak, the over 5,000 CSOs could become an important force in generating demand for efficient and transparent procurement, but there is no CSO with a primary focus on procurement.[13]

To play their roles effectively, CSOs must have the right, the tools, the organization, and the skills to do so, but these prerequisites are far from being met uniformly across the region. Several countries still do not have adequate legislation granting citizens access to information. For example, Guatemala does not have implementing regulations that govern public access to information; access is a constitutional right, but because of the lack of regulations its interpretation is arbitrary.[14]

Effective civil society oversight also requires that governments generate and regularly disseminate reliable and relevant information on their budgets and that the reports issued are easily understood by the general public. The governments of Brazil, Chile, Mexico, and Paraguay post budget, procurement, and accounting information on their Web sites, but the public often cannot interrogate the systems to produce user-friendly reports, the degree of technological literacy needed to access the information is beyond that prevalent in some countries, and e-procurement systems still typically cover only a small fraction of the transactions. There is, however, some good news. In Mexico, for example, a federal law to promote the activities of CSOs formalizes their participation, and such participation has taken numerous forms. In Honduras, an innovative partnership has been established between citizens and the SAI to undertake a form of joint audits (see box 1.2). In Colombia, there is advanced legislation on the matter (see box 3.5 in chapter 3). And in Peru civil society is active and some groups are very sophisticated (see box 3.6 in chapter 3).

---

**Box 1.2**

## Honduras: Citizen Participation in Audit Oversight

The supreme audit institution of Honduras, Tribunal Superior de Cuentas (TSC), recently undertook a pilot program aimed at involving citizens in its audit engagements. These joint exercises, called "articulated" audits, were carried out in eight institutions (two public hospitals, one school, one university, two municipalities, one road construction project, and one environmental public agency). The articulated audits incorporated citizen complaints into their scope of work as well as more formal information from citizen-led social monitoring exercises. Citizens were also invited to participate in local public meetings with TSC officials so they could put forward concerns and information about the institutions to be audited. Overall, citizen feedback helped to detect irregularities totaling $1.7 million and to identify 47 potential cases of administrative wrongdoing, along with three potential cases of criminal wrongdoing. The audited institutions agreed to implement an action plan based on recommendations put forth by the TSC, and the plan will be monitored by citizens and civil society organizations.

*Source:* Tribunal Superior de Cuentas (TSC).

## Legislatures

All legislatures in the countries reviewed conduct a spirited debate of the proposed budget, largely focusing on their political positions rather than on substance. With the exception of Jamaica, the only parliamentary democracy in the countries reviewed, at the time of their assessment none of the countries was performing adequate legislative oversight of public spending. In addition, their review of the annual reports was typically perfunctory. Legislators asked few detailed questions, and they initiated virtually no follow-up to correct deficiencies identified in the auditor's report.

This general ineffectiveness arises largely from two factors. The first is political. In democratic societies worldwide, when the interests of the legislative majorities and the executive coincide there is generally little incentive for the legislative majorities to find wrongdoing in the executive. The second is resources. Legislators in the countries reviewed have sparse budgetary resources to spend on staff or to acquire the expertise needed to advise on technical issues. Thus their ability to debate technical budget issues, even absent political bias, is severely constrained.

When these factors are taken in conjunction with SAIs that are still struggling to fulfill their mandates and the absence of significant oversight by civil society, it becomes clear that a key pillar in any balanced system of accountability—effective, independent oversight of the executive—remains almost nonexistent across the region.

## Decentralization

Over the last decade and a half, many countries in the LAC region have pursued political, fiscal, and administrative decentralization. According to World Bank data, subnational expenditures now represent approximately 25 percent of total public spending in the region, with this figure rising to as high as 48 percent in Argentina. Arguably, however, full realization of the benefits of decentralization depends on strong subnational procurement, financial management, and administrative capacity.

Yet in the countries reviewed, subnational capacity has not kept pace with the rate of decentralization, and, in fact, many subnational entities cannot justify having, at a most basic level, full-time procurement, budget, or accounting officers. In addition, all of the specific challenges just discussed become steeper with decentralization. There is less automation and integration of information systems and therefore less timely loop-back on the performance of programs; the multiplicity of procurement regimes increases; and holistic internal control frameworks give way to inefficient ex ante checks at the transaction level—all of which complicate the exercise of independent oversight.

Recognizing weak subnational administration as a major constraint, countries such as Brazil and Peru have developed training programs for subnational staff, but, even when these exist, they typically focus on compliance with legal formalities and not on issues of operational efficiency or effectiveness. It can thus be argued that, pending the development of fully capable administrations, civil society organizations could play a role in ensuring that citizens obtain the benefit of programs approved by the legislature and for which budget appropriations have been made. And yet despite the large number of CSOs that exist across the region and work on budget and procurement issues, there is a limited capacity for oversight. Knowledge of resource allocation and procurement processes is technically specialized, and there is no evidence of a concerted effort to organize and train civil society or local communities accordingly.

## A Revitalized Focus Going Forward

In the years since completion of the Country Financial Accountability Assessments and Country Procurement Assessment Reports that underpin this book, several countries have furthered their PFM reform programs. For example, Paraguay has developed more robust budget and accounting systems, which are now being implemented across the public sector. Elsewhere, Honduras and the Dominican Republic have introduced new or upgraded information systems, and both governments are also addressing the need to upgrade independent oversight functions.

Important improvements also have taken place in public procurement. Awareness seems to be growing of the importance of procurement as a strategic function that can, among other things, improve the quality of public expenditures. The procurement function itself is no longer perceived as being a purely administrative one, but rather as a highly specialized, knowledge-based discipline that includes management of a complex process in a sophisticated marketplace. In Panama, for example, the legislature passed a new procurement law, and the government adopted implementing regulations and comprehensive procurement strategies and significantly strengthened the procurement policy directorate. Other countries are reassessing their procurement policies and strategies in order to align them with government economic development plans (Mexico, Peru). In Colombia, the government recently overhauled and modernized the procurement law. In other countries, discrete interventions, initially requiring relatively small regulatory and institutional changes, have proven catalytic to larger systemic reforms and important cultural and behavioral changes (e.g., improvements in efficiency and transparency driven by the strategic use of technology such as in the Brazilian state of Minas Gerais and in Chile). Finally, the majority of countries in the region have implemented e-procurement solutions, ranging from systems that simply publish procurement information to systems that are fully transactional. However, a major challenge lies ahead in promoting reforms that not only address technological constraints but also are transformative in terms of moving from a compliance-with-rules culture to a performance-and-results focus.

Of the countries reviewed, Chile performs better than the rest, with demonstrable impacts. Its success in improving the efficiency and effectiveness of government operations has enabled it (1) to deliver enhanced services to its citizens based on a clear understanding among public sector managers of the government's strategic priorities and predictable cash flows; (2) to strengthen the business climate based on shared confidence that the government's policies are predictable and its actions consistently support those priorities (Chilean companies have therefore become competitive suppliers and credible borrowers in international markets); and (3) to borrow on the international capital markets based on an investment-grade rating derived from confidence that the country's finances are sound and that comprehensive information on government operations is publicly available.

Other LAC countries could learn from Chile's experience in charting out a second wave of reforms. Such reforms should strongly focus first on improving performance and achieving acceptable results within the executive branch and then on strengthening external independent oversight arrangements in the following priority areas:

- Streamlining and simplifying the regulations governing public procurement to enhance economy, efficiency, and competition in public spending;
- Creating and maintaining a professional cadre of procurement staff with cutting-edge skills, such as in supply chain management, who can support a government objective of achieving value for money;
- Improving budget execution reporting so that timely information is available on all government expenditures, national and subnational, in a manner that enhances the monitoring and evaluation of, and opportune adjustments to, the implementation of approved programs;

- Developing robust internal controls, including internal auditing arrangements, so that these controls can provide reasonable assurance about achievement of the government's objectives and support prompt remedial action through early feedback;
- Strengthening and empowering independent oversight (legislatures, auditor generals, and civil society) to make it possible to take corrective action, to make those accountable accept responsibility, to obtain compensation, and, as a result, to enhance government legitimacy, both domestically and internationally.

For those undertaking such reforms, countries worldwide that have implemented or are implementing successful reforms offer important lessons to be kept in mind. First, reform programs should be country-owned and -led with sustained support from senior leadership. Second, it is important to adopt a consultative and inclusive process in agreeing on policy changes. Third, the sequence and timing of steps in any reform program is important. Fourth, and, most important of all, countries should aim first to get the basics right.

## Notes

1. The World Development Indicators Database is not available to the public. All dollars amounts are U.S. dollars unless otherwise indicated.
2. "Poverty" refers to the proportion of the population living on less than $2 per day.
3. Jamaica, Panama, and Costa Rica: ministries of finance; Brazil: Economist Intelligence Unit data.
4. "Legitimacy" is defined in *Latin American Economic Outlook 2008* (OECD 2007) as the confidence people place in fiscal policy as measured by the percentage of respondents who trust that money from taxes is being well spent by the government.
5. Economist Intelligence Unit quarterly data for "world commodity forecasts" and crude oil.
6. These countries include Argentina, Brazil, Chile, and Mexico, where the objectives are typically to protect or enhance safety net programs, or to invest in infrastructure as a way of creating jobs in the short term while laying a foundation for increased productivity and growth in the longer term.
7. American Recovery and Reinvestment Act of 2009 (http://www.recovery.gov).
8. See Corporación Latinobarómetro (2008) for all data in this paragraph. The survey was based on 20,204 interviews conducted between September 1 and October 11, 2008, in 18 Latin American countries.

9. PEFA is a partnership comprising the World Bank, European Commission, U.K. Department for International Development, Swiss State Secretariat for Economic Affairs, Royal Norwegian Ministry of Foreign Affairs, French Ministry of Foreign Affairs, and International Monetary Fund.

10. As an example, of the 10 countries reviewed, 4—Brazil, Colombia, Costa Rica, and Guatemala—had legislatures in which more than 10 political parties were represented.

11. Many countries have adopted the Calvo Doctrine, formulated in the second half of the nineteenth century, which in essence protects them from intervention by foreign governments in legal disputes with their nationals. An extension of this doctrine precludes foreign firms from arbitrating disputes and requires that such disputes be submitted to local courts.

12. Budget classifications are a compilation of the programs for which resources have been allocated. A chart of accounts is the basis on which transactions are compiled, together with the rules for recording those transactions.

13. However, CSOs such as Paricipación Ciudadana, Fundación Institucionalidad y Justicia, and Fundación Solidaridad have produced important work on procurement and transparency, even though their focus is on broader governance and democracy issues.

14. In December 2005, the government of Guatemala issued an *Acuerdo Gubernativo* on General Norms for Access to Public Information, which sets out the obligation for government agencies to furnish information within 30 days. However, the *Acuerdo* does not establish any sanction for those who do not comply.

CHAPTER 2

# Findings from the Country Financial Accountability Assessments

This chapter sets out the main findings from the review of the Country Financial Accountability Assessments. CFAAs evaluate performance by reference to processes and institutional arrangements for the management of public finances, but they do not evaluate how strengths and weaknesses in those processes and institutional arrangements affect the quality of public expenditures. This book attempts to do so by referring to the framework laid out in the World Bank's *Public Expenditure Management Handbook* (World Bank 1998). This framework posits that effective public expenditure management (PEM) should produce favorable outcomes at three levels: (1) aggregate fiscal discipline; (2) resource allocation based on strategic priorities; and (3) efficient and effective delivery of programs and services.

The framework argues that, although aggregate fiscal discipline tends to be addressed and resolved first, followed by issues related to resource allocation and then efficiency and effectiveness, there are in fact substantial interdependencies among the three levels, often making it necessary to address deficiencies at all levels simultaneously in order not to undermine progress at one level. In fact, the *Handbook* holds that "a lack of discipline and budgetary realism in making strategic policy choices leads to a mismatch between policies and resources, resulting in inadequate funding for

23

operations." Put another way, a prerequisite for attaining quality in the use of public resources is that countries successfully implement programs to make progress at all three levels.

The following sections are an analytical discussion of public financial management in the LAC region. The first section summarizes global developments over the last 20 years in accounting, reporting, and auditing. The next section summarizes the status of accounting, reporting, and auditing in the LAC region, which allows a comparison of progress within the region against global trends. The last three sections of this chapter analyze how the LAC countries reviewed have addressed the principal elements of aggregate fiscal discipline, strategic resource allocation, and efficient and effective delivery of services and programs. Each section concludes with a table that sets out the authors' judgments of country performance on each of the three principal levels just listed.

## Recent Global Developments in Accounting, Reporting, and Auditing

The accounting and auditing professions and PFM arrangements have undergone substantial changes over the last 20 years.

Emerging markets recognized the need to address issues of financial discipline following a series of financial crises in the 1980s in which large U.S. and European banks faced potential losses on sovereign debt. They therefore submitted to the use of Brady Bonds. In exchange for the bonds, they were required to adopt domestic economic reforms, with a special emphasis on policies that could reverse capital flight.[2] Such policies included addressing inflation, fully implementing tax policies, committing to fiscal discipline, and taking steps to improve the efficiency of the public sector (Pastor 1990).

In the United States, changes were made early in this century to restore the credibility of the profession and to raise standards of corporate governance following the substantial losses incurred by investors and lenders after the technology bubble burst and major corporate scandals surfaced.[1]

In the European Union, several factors, including the introduction of the euro, the accession of the first wave of Eastern European countries, and the easing of trade barriers across countries, created a need to harmonize the elements of accountability and governance across the community.

As a result of these developments, there has been significant global progress in strengthening the accounting and auditing professions, including in the following respects:

- The *Financial Accounting Advisory Board (FASB)* sets and disseminates the accounting standards used in the U.S. Generally Accepted Accounting Principles (US GAAP). FASB's functions include: (1) improving the usefulness of financial reporting; (2) keeping the standards current; (3) revising the standards to address deficiencies in financial reporting; and (4) promoting international convergence of accounting standards (FASB 2007). Over the last 10 years, FASB has been revising old standards or issuing new ones aimed at reflecting the variety of new financial products developed during this period. In view of the importance of the U.S. financial markets, FASB-related developments have generally driven changes in global accounting practices.

- The *International Accounting Standards Board (IASB)* was founded in 2001 seeking "to provide the world's integrating capital markets with a common language for financial reporting" (IASB 2007). IASB is the overseer and developer of the International Financial Reporting Standards (IFRS), and it sets the standards and issues the interpretations for their implementation. IASB replaced the International Accounting Standards Committee (IASC), which had operated between 1973 and 2001. In April 2001, IASB adopted all International Accounting Standards (IAS) previously issued by IASC and continued their development, calling the new standards International Financial Reporting Standards. In 2002 the EU passed regulations to adopt IFRS for listed companies, effective 2005. This action included reaffirmation of the EU's Fourth Directive (originally adopted in 1978), which specified, among other things, the contents, layouts, valuation rules, and dissemination requirements for annual reporting, and its Seventh Directive (originally adopted in 1983), which specified the main rules and amendments applicable for consolidated accounts. In 2006 IASB and FASB agreed to a roadmap for convergence of IFRS and US GAAP (IASB 2007). Adoption of IFRS was also a condition of EU accession for the Eastern European countries that had applied for admission.

- The *International Federation of Accountants (IFAC)* was established in 1977 to strengthen the worldwide accountancy profession by, among other things, developing high-quality international standards and supporting their adoption and use. In addition to providing a forum for professional exchanges among accountants, IFAC has developed, disseminated, and kept current, standards on ethics for accountants; accounting education; and auditing and assurance. More important from the perspective of this book, IFAC is the parent organization of the International Public Sector Accounting Standards Board (IPSASB), whose goal is to serve the public interest by developing high-quality International Public Sector Accounting Standards (IPSAS) for use by public sector entities in the preparation of general-purpose financial statements. To date, it has issued over 20 international public sector accounting standards (IFAC 2007b).

- The *International Organisation of Supreme Audit Institutions (INTOSAI)* is an umbrella organization of government external auditors. Founded in 1953, the organization "has provided an institutionalised framework for supreme audit institutions to promote development and transfer of knowledge, improve government auditing worldwide and enhance professional capacities, standing and influence of member SAIs in their respective countries."[3] INTOSAI's Ninth Congress in Lima, Peru, in October 1977 adopted the Lima Declaration of Guidelines on Auditing Precepts (INTOSAI 1977). This declaration was reaffirmed and reissued by the secretary general of INTOSAI in Vienna in 1998 and still serves as the essential reference on government auditing.

- The *International Monetary Fund (IMF)* issued the "Government Finance Statistics Manual 2001" (GFS), which it described as "an internationally recognized statistical reporting framework" (IMF 2001). The GFS framework provides a basis for analyzing public investments using a common language so that fiscal analysts can take a consistent approach to handling complex operations that create challenges in fiscal reporting and analysis.

- *International capital markets* now rely heavily on the major rating agencies (e.g., Moody's, Standard & Poors, and Fitch) to assess the credit risk related to fixed-income securities. Countries attaining investment-grade ratings are able to sell sovereign debt to a wide array of institutional investors, and because private borrowers generally cannot support a higher investment rating than their countries, countries that attain investment-grade ratings create a favorable investment climate for their private sectors (Moody's Investors Services 2008). To achieve investment-grade ratings, countries now need to provide accurate, reliable, and comprehensive financial reports that demonstrate, among other things, efficiency in their public spending.

- *A worldwide standards and codes initiative* was launched by the World Bank and the International Monetary Fund in 1999 as a part of an effort to strengthen the international financial architecture following the emerging market crises of the 1990s. The initiative was designed to promote greater financial stability both within countries and internationally through the development, dissemination, and adoption of international standards and codes. The initiative, which involves an assessment of individual countries, is undertaken by the World Bank or the IMF, and its outcome is a Report on the Observance of Standards and Codes (ROSC). The initiative covers 12 areas, one of which is accounting and auditing (ROSC A&A).[4] So far, 16 ROSC A&A reviews have been conducted in the LAC region.[5]

## Status of Accounting, Reporting, and Auditing in the Region

The present PFM arrangements in the LAC countries were influenced by the cultural, legal, and political heritage of colonization. On the legal side, the systems used in Latin American and Francophone countries originated in Napoleonic or Roman law (civil law) in which rules are codified and prescriptive, and procedural formalities have traditionally been observed rather strictly.[6] This framework was further reinforced by the nature of the LAC region economies: agriculture- and commodities-based, with small elites owning large holdings. In turn, the management of these holdings was usually delegated to an administrative cadre (see Nef 2003). In this context, the role of accounting was to count product and record sales and units of production. To keep the function simple, rules were codified and seldom modified, a custom that has persisted to date. Although the region's former British colonies, typically the Caribbean countries, inherited Britain's Westminster model, the observance of fiscal discipline and the performance of PFM systems and practices in these countries have not evolved differently from those of the Latin American countries.[7] Finally, because of the region's proximity to the United States, it is perhaps not surprising that some U.S. impacts are evident. Over the last 40 years what has emerged is a hybrid home-grown plus US GAAP model that, though presenting challenges to companies wishing to list on U.S. capital markets, nevertheless can serve to facilitate future convergence with IFRS.

This legacy is formidable. Completed ROSC A&A reviews confirm that accounting in the LAC countries has largely remained a bookkeeping function performed by practitioners who learned their trade in high school or university, following nonstandardized curricula. The ROSC A&A reviews also indicate that coverage of both public and private sector accounting theory and practice is scarce in university curricula and, even when available, is poorly taught. The downstream consequence is that an insufficient number of practitioners who are poorly trained enter the profession. Furthermore, few countries rely on a special exam for entry into the profession, and, although some countries acknowledge the need to refresh practitioners' skills, the availability of continuing professional education is extremely limited. This situation contrasts with that in most OECD countries, where accounting is a professional function, with standardized entrance exams, and practitioners are required to undergo continuing professional education. Moreover, although the organic accounting law may make reference to IFRS or US GAAP, few of the countries have standards that approach those currently in use in OECD countries. More important, the LAC ROSC A&A program confirms that these laws and standards are seldom updated.[8] By contrast, as described earlier, IFRS are continually updated to take account of changing circumstances and new financing techniques.[9]

The LAC ROSC A&A program also reveals that auditing in the region is still viewed largely as a compliance function. The profession is again different in OECD countries, where the focus is now on efficient and effective management of resources. Among the LAC countries, the main qualification for becoming an auditor is having practiced as an accountant for a number of years. There is no special educational requirement or entrance exam, and, more important, these countries tend to not have a detailed code of ethics governing issues of independence and integrity of auditors.[10]

How then do accounting, reporting, and auditing today in the LAC countries reviewed compare with the global professional architecture that has evolved? An assessment can be made along the following dimensions:

- INTOSAI lists 187 member countries, which include every country in the LAC region.

• In 2005 nearly 7,000 listed companies in 25 countries were using IFRS. Of these, only Brazil and Chile in the LAC region had established timelines to adopt or converge to IFRS (IASB 2007). More encouraging, the ROSC A&A program indicates that most countries have based their national accounting standards on a version of US GAAP or IFRS. However, although US GAAP and IFRS are dynamic and are constantly being amended to take account of new financial developments or to address gaps in the coverage of accounting systems, the LAC countries have tended to adopt static national standards.

• As of September 2007, 10 countries had adopted IPSAS, and another 55 were in various stages of planning or implementing IPSAS. In addition, the five major Anglophone governments (Australia, Canada, New Zealand, United Kingdom, United States) had adopted national accrual accounting systems that were similar to IPSAS (IFAC 2007c). In the LAC region, however, only Argentina, Barbados, Cayman Islands, El Salvador, Jamaica, Peru, and Uruguay have committed themselves to and are in various stages of implementing IPSAS.

• Worldwide, 87 countries or national jurisdictions have attained investment-grade ratings from Moody's.[11] These include all countries that have recently acceded to the EU, the major emerging market (BRICS) countries, and most of the newly industrialized countries of East Asia.[12] In the LAC region, the countries with investment-grade ratings are Brazil, Chile, Costa Rica, El Salvador, Mexico, Panama, Peru, and St. Vincent and the Grenadines (Brazil and Peru attained their investment-grade ratings in 2008).

Thus when viewed against the global developments in accounting and auditing over the last 20 years, it is clear that the region is only now beginning to catch up, driven by the effects of growing globalization and recognition of the benefits of adopting internationally recognized auditing and accounting standards in both the public and private sectors.

There is, however, widespread awareness of the imperative to catch up. During the 2007 CReCER conference in Mexico City, Chilean and Costa Rican participants shared the benefits accruing to their economies as a result of adopting international financial reporting standards.[13] At the follow-on 2008 conference held in San Salvador, Brazilian participants also acknowledged the considerable benefits that had accrued to their country as a result of adopting international financial reporting standards. Such benefits included the fact that in 2007 FDI flows rose by 46 percent in the LAC region, reaching a record of $106 billion, of which some 81 percent of the increase accrued to just three countries–Brazil, Chile, and Mexico— all of which have investment-grade ratings and are at the high end of PFM performance, as the rest of this chapter will demonstrate (ECLAC 2008).

## Aggregate Fiscal Discipline

The essence of aggregate fiscal discipline is that government spending is closely aligned with what is affordable over the medium term and, in turn, with the annual budget. Key aspects of PFM that determine success or failure in this area are satisfactory PFM legal and institutional frameworks, comprehensive national budgets, and the application of hard budget constraints when formulating those budgets.

### Legal and Institutional Frameworks

The CFAAs confirmed that the PFM legal and institutional frameworks in the LAC countries were largely satisfactory. All countries either had or were in the process of enacting mandates for the budget process. Normative laws were also in place setting out the various responsibilities for PFM. In some countries, such as Brazil, Chile, Colombia, Costa Rica, Jamaica, and Panama, the needed laws and regulations had been in place for several years. In others, such as Guatemala and Paraguay, new laws and regulations had been established more recently. In the Dominican Republic and Honduras, new laws and regulations were being developed at the time of the CFAA. In general, these laws and regulations were satisfactory, although some need updating while others need amendment to address gaps and inconsistencies. At the same time, and central to the achievement of aggregate fiscal discipline, some countries, including Brazil, Chile, Colombia, and Panama, had adopted fiscal responsibility laws or their equivalent. All 10 CFAAs reported that governments were committed to operating within a balanced budget, but only in Brazil and Chile was there substantial progress in embedding the pursuit of aggregate financial discipline into central government operations.

### Budget Comprehensiveness

In principle, all resources allocated for recurrent operations and capital investments should be channeled through the budget and thus be subject to review by both the executive and legislative branches of government. In addition, capital investments should be subject to a screening process to establish their economic merit.

In theory, most countries of the region had budget systems that covered the entire central government, with autonomous agencies being included on a net (or summarized) basis. On that basis, the allocation of all public resources should have been broadly open to scrutiny. In reality, off-budget accounts continue to be a problem in many countries, especially in Costa Rica and Argentina. In some countries, notably Paraguay and Guatemala, the CFAAs indicated that autonomous organizations did not report their net results to the government.

Another issue was the nontransparent budgetary mechanisms that commit public resources to programs without legislative scrutiny, or cause public funds to be spent on the basis of discretionary decisions. Included in the former category are Chile's use of profits from the national copper company (which is not included in the budget) to finance activities of its Ministry of Defense (also not included in the budget); Jamaica's use of letters of comfort, issued by the executive without prior approval of the legislature, that obligate the government to make good on a loan contracted by a public or private third party if the latter defaults; and the Colombian practice of using earmarks to preallocate future budgetary resources. In all cases in which authorized budgets substantially exceeded available cash, the treasury used cash rationing to determine what received funding, and cash allocations were often based on the government's political priorities instead of the purposes approved by legislatures.

The final issue related to budget comprehensiveness is still evident in some of the larger federal countries: the coverage of budget transfers to subnational governments.[14] Transfers are included in the national government's budget, but information on how the regional authority receiving the transfer spent those funds is usually not included in the national budget.[15] Thus it is difficult to ensure that transferred funds are allocated to the intended program, and even more difficult to verify that the funds, allocated to support priority national programs, were actually spent for the purpose intended.

How these exceptions to the principle of comprehensive budget coverage are handled is revealing about a country's attitude toward fiscal discipline. For example, although Chile explicitly excludes its Ministry of Defense and its national copper company from its budget and accounting systems, both the Ministry of Defense and the copper company report their results on a net basis to parliament, and those reports are reasonably comprehensive. Brazil's executive branch takes aggregate fiscal discipline very seriously, and it makes a determined effort to devise accurate revenue forecasts to serve as a hard constraint on a carefully derived spending program. Until recently, Argentina had very few off-budget accounts. At the height of the 2002 economic crisis, the government created some off-budget accounts as a means of protecting favored programs from the broad budget cuts imposed by the government. Since then, although the country has largely recovered from the crisis, the number of off-budget activities has increased year by year. Guatemala had many off-budget activities that were not consolidated in its budget and did not provide summarized results. In Paraguay, the government's two largest cash generators are not integrated into the budget.[16] Although Colombia has few off-budget agencies, it protects the flow of resources to favored activities through the extensive use of earmarks. All other countries use off-budget accounts to some degree.

### Hard Budget Constraints
The final critical element of aggregate fiscal discipline is that resource allocation must be subject to a hard constraint—that is, cash availability to cover projected expenditures must be firmly established on the basis of well-developed forecasts.

The LAC countries need to improve the accuracy of the revenue forecasting side of the equation. To do so, they must develop the political will needed to make accurate forecasts, even if those forecasts would limit the resources available for spending. Achieving those forecasts implies upgrading staff capacity and the systems used for forecasting revenues. At best, routine overestimations of revenue constrain the individual agencies with unpredictable availability of cash; at worst, public resources are allocated according to the discretionary decisions of the executive instead of according to the policies articulated and approved in the budget. Chile, Costa Rica, Guatemala, and Panama have invested considerable effort in developing sustainable revenue estimates, and these forecasts provide the needed hard constraint. Brazil's revenue forecasts, which normally are well formulated within the executive branch, are undermined during legislative consideration of the budget. The other countries have considerable room to improve their revenue forecasting, and therefore they lack the hard constraint that is a prerequisite for aggregate fiscal discipline.

### Level 1 Summary
Table 2.1 indicates how all the countries in the sample perform on the primary elements of aggregate fiscal discipline. An effective legal and institutional framework is a key component of aggregate fiscal discipline, and

**Table 2.1    Level 1: Aggregate Fiscal Discipline**

| Issue | Brazil | Chile | Colombia | Costa Rica | Dom. Rep. | Guatemala | Honduras | Jamaica | Panama | Paraguay |
|---|---|---|---|---|---|---|---|---|---|---|
| Legal and institutional framework | 1 | 1 | 1 | 1 | 3 | 1 | 2 | 2 | 1 | 2 |
| Comprehensiveness of the budget | 1 | 1 | 2 | 2 | 3 | 3 | 3 | 2 | 2 | 3 |
| Hard budget constraint | 2 | 1 | 3 | 2 | 3 | 2 | 3 | 3 | 2 | 3 |

*Note:* 1 = adequate or above; 2 = could benefit from strengthening; 3 = weak; empty cell = nothing reported in CFAA. These ratings reflect a qualitative judgment based on the subjective diagnosis presented in the CFAAs.

most LAC countries either have or are in the process of developing satisfactory frameworks. In addition, most of the region's governments have policies that articulate a commitment to fiscal discipline. However, although these qualities are necessary ingredients of aggregate fiscal discipline, they are not sufficient to promote good outcomes. Also necessary is comprehensive budget coverage and hard budget constraints. Within the LAC region, only Chile and Brazil have comprehensive budgets that are capped by hard constraints. Countries that rely on extrabudgetary approaches or that do not use hard budget constraints frequently allocate more resources to selected programs than can be supported from government revenues. As a result, those programs receive cash as and when the government realizes revenues. Meanwhile, it is difficult to hold individual agency managers accountable for the outcomes of their programs when the resources they need are provided at irregular intervals or in unpredictable amounts.

## Strategic Resource Allocation

Prioritizing competing claims on scarce resources is fundamentally a political exercise in which politicians set priorities based on their understanding of the preferences of their key constituencies. It is therefore critical that the executive provide a rationale for the policy priorities it has chosen and the related resource implications. PFM aspects critical to success in this area are clear articulation of strategic priorities, a participatory approach to budgeting, and use of a multiyear planning process.

Another important element of strategic resource allocation is the compilation of timely, accurate information to enable monitoring of how allocated resources were actually spent. Throughout the sampled countries, budget execution reporting is generally a component of broader elec-tronic systems for accounting, reporting, and auditing, which are used mainly for oversight of government operations and monitoring govern-ment services. An analytical discussion of budget execution reporting appears later in this chapter.

### Clear Articulation of Strategic Priorities

On a broad level, adopting a rational approach to allocating limited resources according to strategic priorities is a difficult task for poor coun-tries, where governments attempt to address overwhelming unmet social needs with meager increments of resources (Schick 1998). This effort is even more difficult in the LAC region with its political structures of centralized republics and a tradition of legislatures controlled by the president's party. In such a situation, politicians have de facto discretion in allocating public resources and face limited accountability in how those resources are spent. In turn, an enabling environment is created within which public sector managers work to protect politically pre-ferred programs, either by creating off-budget accounts or by using other nontransparent mechanisms.

Chile does an effective job of allocating public resources according to strategic priorities. Brazil has a four-year plan, the *Plano Plurianual de Acao*, in which each incoming administration sets out its strategic priori-ties for the period covered. However, the widespread use of earmarks, many constitutionally mandated, undermines implementation of the gov-ernment's strategic priorities.[17] In Paraguay, rather than being a tool for planning, prioritization, and disciplined resource allocation, the budget is frequently an obstacle to effective public expenditure management, because it is a rigid set of instructions that often provide contradictory incentives (World Bank 2006f).

### Participatory Budgeting

Although all countries in the sample have well-articulated budget for-mulation and execution frameworks, Chile and Brazil use the most par-ticipatory processes when viewed from the perspective of agency and civil society participation in the budget process. In both countries, the central agencies play a major role in defining and selecting the policies and programs that meet the government's strategic priorities, and thus have broad ownership of those resource allocations. Costa Rica, Colombia, and Panama have budget processes that are similarly participatory; the central agencies formulate the programs to be financed through the budget. In Paraguay and Guatemala, the budget systems also involve substantial communications between the country's ministry of finance, which decides the contents of the country's budget, and the sector agencies, which are responsible for formulating and implementing the government's programs. Because Jamaica's budget has exceedingly limited headroom, individual agencies have only limited influence on the decision-making process. Honduras and the Dominican Republic have begun implementing improvements to their budget processes to make them more rational and participatory.

The LAC region also has experienced recent progress in increasing CSO participation in the budget formulation process. For example, CSOs and the press worked together to urge the government of Guyana to address the issues raised in the CFAA (see box 3.1 in chapter 3.) Many CSOs are increasingly weighing in on budget choices, and many governments are acknowledging the fact that CSO participation lends legitimacy and credibility. Recently, the Open Budget Project of the International Budget Program, a U.S.-based CSO, organized other CSOs in 85 countries to review and assess the effectiveness and transparency of the processes used to allocate resources. Not only has this effort resulted in an independent ranking of budget processes, but the project has also helped upgrade the technical capacity of the participating CSOs.

Despite the large number of CSOs across the region working on budget issues, their capacity to provide oversight of national government units in remote locations or among subnational government units is limited. Knowledge of resource allocation processes is technically specialized, and few people or programs are available to train CSOs at the district or community levels. To play their roles effectively, CSOs also must have the right to see and review budgets, but several countries still do not have adequate legislation granting citizens access to information. For example, Guatemala does not have regulated public access to information—access is a constitutional right, but the lack of regulation makes its interpretation arbitrary.[18] Without a clear legal framework that requires government officials to provide the public with information or to respond to requests, civil society finds monitoring difficult. Even when there is a legal basis, and therefore rules for access to information, under some circumstances public officials can be arbitrary in their compliance with these rules. Effective civil society oversight also requires governments to generate and regularly disseminate reliable and relevant information on their budgets and accounts. Reports must be easy to understand by those not proficient in financial matters. Even though many governments (Brazil, Chile, Mexico, Paraguay) post budget and accounting information on their Web sites, the public often cannot interrogate the system to produce user-friendly reports, and the degree of technological literacy needed to access the information may be beyond the capabilities of many citizens or CSOs.

## Multiyear Planning

An important factor in ensuring that resources are allocated according to strategic priorities is the use of medium-term plans that combine investment and recurrent cost data for preexisting, ongoing, and future government programs. Such an approach enables an evaluation of costs against impacts and informed decision making about which programs should be supported and the extent of such support. Ideally, a robust medium-term expenditure framework feeds a multiyear budget.

None of the countries reviewed used a well-developed medium-term expenditure framework, and very few provided budgets extending beyond one year. About half of the countries produced multiyear plans of some sort.[19] Of those, few produced annual budgets or even investment programs based on their multiyear plans. In addition, although investment projects formulated in the context of a government's multiyear plan normally receive economically based scrutiny, other investments were included in the budget independent of the planning process and generally did not receive the same scrutiny. Thus they could not be certified as high priority or economically justifiable.

When medium-term plans were produced, few provided the sort of information that would enable the evaluation of past or ongoing programs. Of those that did provide cost and outcome information on future investments, there was ample room for improvement. Chile uses a four-year plan that is updated twice a year and based on sectoral planning exercises, which, in turn, enable line ministries to make strategic choices. The plan includes aggregate costs and targets, but it lacks detail and does not inform the budget. It takes into account new projects, but the extent to which it takes into account ongoing programs is not clear. Brazil develops a four-year plan at the beginning of each administration. Within broad sectoral parameters, the plan guides budget preparation for the intervening years. Colombia's investment plan is the product of a good effort at an aggregate level. Panama has a five-year planning exercise that is formulated at an aggregate level and enables ceilings to be set for the overall

**Table 2.2    Level 2: Strategic Resource Allocation**

| Issue | Brazil | Chile | Colombia | Costa Rica | Dom. Rep. | Guatemala | Honduras | Jamaica | Panama | Paraguay |
|---|---|---|---|---|---|---|---|---|---|---|
| Clearly articulated strategic priorities | 1 | 1 | 2 | 2 | 3 | 2 | 3 | 3 | 2 | 3 |
| Participatory budgeting | 1 | 1 | 2 | 2 | 3 | 2 | 3 | 2 | 2 | 2 |
| Multiyear planning | 2 | 2 | 2 | 3 | 3 | 3 | 3 | 3 | 2 | 3 |
| Accurate, timely, and comprehensive budget execution and monitoring information | 2 | 1 | 3 | 2 | 3 | 2 | 3 | 3 | 2 | 2 |

*Note:* 1 = adequate or above; 2 = could benefit from strengthening; 3 = weak; empty cell = nothing reported in CFAA. These ratings reflect a qualitative judgment based on the subjective diagnosis presented in the CFAAs.

budget. But there is insufficient detail to set ceilings by sector, and not all projects undertaken by the government are screened by the plan.

### Level 2 Summary

Table 2.2 indicates how all the countries in the sample performed relative to the leading dimensions of strategic resource allocation. The strategic allocation of resources requires that government clearly articulate the policy and program priorities that will receive support, and that the individual agencies develop in detail the sector policies and programs within their jurisdictions. Resource allocation decisions can then be made in the context of a multiyear planning framework that considers the full cost and impact of the agencies' proposals, feeding into a multiyear budget. Of the countries in the sample, only Chile and Brazil had processes for clearly articulating strategic priorities and formulating sector policies and programs. None of the countries reviewed had a budget based on a comprehensive multiyear plan. However, virtually all of the countries reviewed had some sort of planning exercise, but only Brazil, Chile, Colombia, and Panama appeared to use the plan for more than vetting specific investments. In summary, weak planning processes make it difficult to determine the impacts investments will have on recurrent costs, and they diminish a government's capacity to increase the efficiency and effectiveness of public spending.

## Efficient and Effective Delivery of Services and Programs

A third key factor in PFM performance is the extent to which public entities produce efficient and effective results in implementing policies and programs and delivering services. In effect, this factor answers the question of whether government spending produces the outputs and outcomes expected at the time the government chose to support the underlying policies and programs. Outcomes in this area illustrate the interdependency among the three levels. The determinants of success are the following:

- Imposing a genuinely hard budget constraint during budget execution;
- Giving legitimacy to policies through the decision-making process;
- Ensuring predictability of funding for approved expenditures–both within the budget year and from one year to the next;
- Delegating authority to line managers to make financial decisions commensurate with independently verifiable accountability for producing outputs and achieving outcomes.

The importance of hard budget constraints was discussed in detail in connection with aggregate fiscal discipline, and the issue of legitimacy has been addressed in connection with strategic priorities and participatory budgeting. This section focuses on the two remaining issues: predictability of funding and delegating authority to line managers. The "delegating authority" issue comprises four major elements: (1) a culture of managing for results; (2) availability of budget execution information in order to manage appropriately; (3) effective internal control and audit frameworks; and (4) independent oversight arrangements.

### Predictability of Funding

This issue is related to the extent to which the treasury allocates funds to individual entities for their programs as needed, according to accurate cash flow projections that are, in turn, based on approved expenditure programs. Chile focuses on such predictability, so that its agencies can make payments as needed. Brazil suffers from overly optimistic revenue forecasts because of legislative amendments to the budgets submitted by the executive, leading to frequent midyear cash rationing. Costa Rica and Panama have good systems for providing funds to their agencies, but ex ante controls imposed by the SAI constrains the timeliness of the actual release of cash. Colombia's cash predictability is limited by the government's practice of using earmarks and commitments to frustrate budget stringencies. Jamaica has a good cash management system, but severe budget constraints make it difficult for the treasury to make cash available as needed. Finally, cash is rationed in the Dominican Republic, Honduras, and Paraguay, so that agencies receive less cash than allocated, on a schedule that is difficult to predict.

## Managing for Results

An important element of efficient public expenditure management is to strike a balance between centralized restraint and flexibility at the individual agency level. In other words, in implementing policies and programs, agencies should be free to deploy predictable cash flows that they consider necessary to produce targeted outcomes, and the central authority should use ex post information to hold each agency accountable for its results.

Of the countries reviewed, only Chile manages effectively for results. In the mid-1990s, the executive and legislative branches agreed that they wanted to implement true PEM reform and thus establish the country's credibility as a trading partner for the United States and the European Union. The government understood the importance of aggregate fiscal discipline and resource allocation according to strategic priorities, and it undertook the needed institutional changes. The government also understood that agencies could not fulfill their roles unless they developed a strong management culture. As a result, today agency heads function as managers. They focus on results and impacts, and they use the data and information available to them, including internal audit findings, to monitor progress on an ongoing basis.

Brazil, too, is moving toward a results management approach. There has been substantial devolution of responsibility for implementing programs, but there is still no real results-based management culture within individual agencies—ex ante controls remain a major instrument for ensuring compliance with rules, cash flow is regular but not always predictable, and the internal audit function has considerable scope for improvement.

Colombia, Costa Rica, and Panama have some very effective PFM systems and practices, but agencies lack both the authority and the capacity to drive the selection of programs, funding is not predictable, and compliance with ex ante controls imposes considerable burdens on managers and attracts undue attention from the countries' external auditors.

A prerequisite of a managing-for-results culture is the availability of robust management information systems as well as monitoring and evaluation regimes. At the resource allocation stage, the central authority uses these tools to establish the allocations and hard caps for selected programs. During implementation, it uses them to monitor progress and assess the performance of agencies. In the resource allocation phase, agencies use these tools to formulate and compare alternative programs and to make choices between them. During the implementation phase, these tools are used to monitor performance and determine what corrections are needed to meet schedules and enhance impacts.

At the agency level, the ability to make appropriate decisions is affected by the quality of available information. At the national level, timely and informative reports were available in Chile, Colombia, and Costa Rica. A challenge, however, is that even in countries with good reporting at the central level, less reliable reports were forthcoming from remote service delivery points or subnational administrative units. This unreliability was cited as an issue in both the Brazil and Colombia CFAAs.

Despite these issues, virtually all of the budget and accounting systems in use among the sample countries were capable of providing adequate management information and monitoring indicators, and some of the newer systems were capable of providing very good information. Brazil, Chile, Colombia, Costa Rica, and Panama were regularly producing monitoring indicators related to the performance of programs and policies. In Chile, these indicators were being used both as inputs to the budget and as management tools by the agencies. The other four countries were using this data mainly for evaluating individual agency performance. The impediments therefore tended to be more managerial than technological—few public sector managers demanded the full range of information that their systems could provide, and which would enable them to manage more effectively.

### Budget Execution Reporting

For effective monitoring of budget execution, information systems must include the following features: (1) the budget is compiled using a system of expenditure classifications that enables monitoring the use of resources allocated for specific purposes; (2) the budget integrates the resource requirements for recurrent costs and capital investments to ensure that the long-term impacts of investments are fully taken into account; (3) expenditure classifications used in the budget are embedded within the chart of accounts; and (4) either through integrated budgeting and accounting or through detailed reporting procedures, the national government is able to monitor the actual use of resources in subnational agencies.

When budgets are compiled according to programmatic classifications, releases are made directly to the intended programs. Among the sample, Brazil, Chile, Costa Rica, and Panama used programmatic budgetary classifications. When administrative classifications are used (resources are allocated at the agency level and then subclassified according to functions), it is difficult to determine whether priority programs received intended levels of funding, unless a program is managed entirely within a single agency. The systems used in Colombia, Guatemala, Honduras, and Paraguay allocated budgetary resources by administrative classification and then within each agency's budget further classified by function and subclassified by program. The Dominican Republic and Jamaica used the administrative and functional classification, resulting in difficulty monitoring execution at the program level.

Capital and recurrent budgets should ideally be integrated in order to provide a comprehensive view of the inputs, outputs, and outcomes of existing and proposed programs. Such an approach allows the longer-term implications of capital expenditures for a government's recurrent budget to be properly evaluated.[20] Brazil, Chile, and Costa Rica integrated their investment and recurrent budgets. In Guatemala, Honduras, Jamaica, Panama, and Paraguay, the budget processes were closely managed by the ministries of finance, which delivered unified investment and recurrent budgets to their legislatures. In Colombia and the Dominican Republic, the investment and recurrent budgets were prepared separately under the direction of individual agencies.

A budget system is a compilation of the programs for which resources have been appropriated and in which the mechanisms for releasing cash to those programs during the year are explicit. An accounting system is a compilation of the transactions made by an entity, together with the rules for recording those transactions. It is easier to ensure that allocations were spent as intended by the budget when both systems are fully aligned or integrated. Of the countries in the sample, only Costa Rica and Panama had budget systems that were fully integrated with the accounting systems. Not only were the budget classifications aligned with the chart of accounts, but entering information in one system automatically entered it into the other. Brazil, Chile, Guatemala, Honduras, and Paraguay had budget and accounting systems that were aligned, but the systems were not integrated. The remaining countries' systems were neither aligned nor integrated, making it difficult to track how budget allocations were actually spent.[21]

A further issue is that it becomes difficult to verify that resources allocated in the budget were spent for the purpose intended when the accounting system of the spending unit is disconnected from the government's centralized budget and accounting system. In addition to the reasons already discussed, such a disconnect also occurs when central government funding is provided through transfers to subnational agencies but subnational agency accounting is not integrated with the national accounting system. In these instances, financial data on the actual use of resources allocated under the budget by subnational agencies cannot be substantiated without additional information. Of the countries in the sample, only Chile integrates the budgets and accounts of subnational agencies in a unified system maintained by its Ministry of the Interior. All of the countries in the sample have subnational spending units whose transactions are not fully integrated with the countries' centralized systems.

### Internal Controls and Internal Auditing

Internal control is the "process designed, implemented and maintained by those charged with governance, management and other personnel to provide reasonable assurance about the achievement of an entity's objectives with regard to reliability of financial reporting, effectiveness and efficiency of operations, and compliance with applicable laws and regulations" (IFAC 2007a).

The control environment is the core of the entire internal control system. It includes the governance and management functions and sets the tone of the government (INTOSAI 2004). Elements of the control environment are the personal and professional integrity and ethical values of the executive and agency staff, a commitment to competence, the executive's philosophy and operating style (i.e., the "tone at the top"), the organizational structure, and human resource policies and practices. When looked at as a whole, tone at the top is critical in determining the performance of the internal control frameworks across the region. Even though other weaknesses in internal control frameworks contribute to weak performance, only negligible improvement is possible in the absence of clear direction for improvement from the top.

Tone-at-the-top issues are rooted in the region's restricted democracies—strong presidencies and weak legislatures (discussed later in this chapter). At the same time, a prevalent culture in which the interests of the owner family are perceived to be the same as the interests of the enterprise, in which administrators give unquestioned loyalty to the family over the enterprise, and in which extended families play a fundamental role in public life, give legislators from the president's party and administrators within the government every incentive to wish to please the president and facilitate the implementation of his or her decisions (Nef 2003). In view of this background, perhaps it is not surprising that the development of formal internal control frameworks, which are aligned with internationally recognized standards, is still in its infancy.

By contrast, and consistent with the legacy of codified rules and procedures discussed earlier, the area in which the LAC countries perform relatively well is the establishment of control activities. These policies and procedures are established to mitigate risk, and they include activities such as documented authorization and approval procedures, segregation of duties, controls over access to resources and records, verifications, and regular reconciliations. Virtually all countries had stipulated control activities, and Brazil, Chile, Costa Rica, and Guatemala had well-designed systems. Some of the gaps included: (1) control activities that were not integrated into the financial system (Paraguay); (2) control activities that were so numerous as to be burdensome on the agencies (Panama); and (3) staff insufficiently skilled to implement the control activities (Honduras).

Nevertheless, except for Chile the internal control function was uniformly weak in practice across the countries reviewed. Most countries supplement or replace weak internal control systems with ex ante controls applied from outside. What differentiates Chile, which has a highly competent internal control function, is that this activity is not viewed as ensuring compliance but rather as producing important management information. A critical mass of suitably qualified staff has been assigned to this function in each agency, and public sector managers have received training in the use of internally generated financial reports that help ensure compliance with the government's rules. A serious interest, in the effective delivery of government services and the efficient utilization of public resources, among leaders of the executive and legislative branches has proven to be the main incentive for Chile's success in this area. By contrast, weaknesses in internal control in the other countries can be traced back to a lesser appreciation for internal controls as a tool for effective management.

Finally, internal controls remain effective only to the extent that there is continuous monitoring to assess performance over time, accompanied by remedial action. Monitoring includes but is not limited to divergent activities such as a review of whether bank reconciliations are prepared on a timely basis or a review of internal audit evaluations. Timely monitoring of results was a feature of integrated control frameworks in Costa Rica and Chile, whereas in the Dominican Republic, Honduras, and Paraguay there was widespread unevenness and gaps.

Internal audit is part of the internal control framework. This function typically enables the executive branch to monitor the effectiveness of those controls.[22] The American Institute of Internal Auditors has developed an internationally recognized definition that describes internal auditing as "an independent, objective assurance and consulting activity designed to add value and improve an organization's operations. It helps an organization accomplish its objectives by bringing a systematic, disciplined approach to evaluate and improve the effectiveness of risk management, control, and governance processes" (IIARF 2004). For an internal audit function to be effective, staff must be as functionally and organizationally independent from management as possible, provided with the appropriate resources to meet organizational needs, able to report to the highest level of authority within the organization, and able to ensure that appropriate and timely actions are taken in response to audit findings. When an internal audit function is effective, it can contribute to the efficiency of the external auditors' work by reducing the nature, scope, or elapsed time of the procedures required for their work.

With the exception of Chile, internal audit is another area of generalized weakness across the region. The reasons for this weakness are inconsistency of standards applied across the function (Honduras, Paraguay), a shortage of suitably qualified staff (Brazil, Dominican Republic, Guatemala, Honduras, Jamaica, Paraguay), insufficient budgetary resources (Colombia and Guatemala), lack of quality control over the internal audit (Colombia, Costa Rica, Paraguay), lack of appreciation for this function among public sector managers, and a lack of authority to follow up and correct deficiencies identified by audits.

Again, what differentiates Chile is that its internal audit units are staffed with adequate numbers of suitably qualified staff, and there is broad appreciation among senior public sector managers that audits can help them improve the agency's effectiveness. Chile's internal auditors work against clear standards that were set by the executive's central council, which also coordinates the activities of the various internal audit units. They also keep their scope of work manageable by using risk-based sampling techniques to determine their areas of focus, while building on the compliance work carried out by agency staff. Finally, internal audit findings are taken seriously, and thus identified deficiencies are addressed.

### Independent Oversight

Any balanced system of accountability must include an independent oversight component consisting of, among other things, an external audit function, civil society oversight, and legislative overview. The role of civil society was addressed earlier, but the roles of the external auditor and the legislature, discussed in this section, are also critical.

An *external audit* is "an indispensable part of a regulatory system whose aim is to reveal deviations from accepted standards and violations of the principles of legality, efficiency, effectiveness and economy of financial management early enough to make it possible to take corrective action in individual cases, to make those accountable accept responsibility, to obtain compensation, or to take steps to prevent—or at least render more difficult—such breaches" (INTOSAI 1977).

The internationally recognized benchmark for assessing the effectiveness of supreme audit institutions is the Lima Declaration of Guidelines on Auditing Precepts, issued by INTOSAI in October 1977 and updated in 1998 (INTOSAI 1977). The declaration contains a comprehensive list of goals and issues related to government auditing. It supports the establishment of an independent government audit functions on the premise that SAIs can accomplish their tasks objectively and effectively only if they are independent of the audited entity and are protected against outside influence.

Overall, the issues of external audit are similar to those of internal audit, only less severe. Each country's SAI serves as the external auditor for government entities. In some countries, the SAI is organized as a court of accounts; in others, the controller general's office is the SAI. To a large extent, these entities perform the same functions regardless of structure, but, according to the CFAAs, they were similarly weak. Nevertheless, in many cases the SAI was well regarded as an institution, and, with a few exceptions, the heads of the SAIs have commanded respect.

As just noted, the chief aim of the Lima Declaration is that the SAI be independent. Specifically, SAIs should have (1) constitutionally enshrined functional and organizational independence; (2) constitutionally enshrined procedures for removing from office members of a decision-making college (court of accounts) or the head of a monocratically organized SAI (controller/auditor general); and (3) the appropriate budget to undertake their responsibilities and to use the funds allocated to them as they see fit. In these respects, the region's SAIs are broadly independent. In most countries, the SAI is appointed by the legislature or a specially constituted legislative committee, and thus the independence test is largely met. However, some responsibilities undertaken by SAIs potentially undermine their independence from, and objectivity toward, auditees. For example, some SAIs are involved in designing and implementing ex ante controls (Costa Rica, Panama), some specify the accounting principles applicable to their country's public sector (Chile and Colombia), and some prepare their country's annual accounts (Chile).

The Lima Declaration also focuses on audit methodology and the capacity of audit staff. Recognizing that audits can rarely be all-inclusive because of resource constraints, the declaration recommends that countries adopt a sampling approach, which in today's context means adopting risk-based methods so that resources can be directed to the most critical areas, and that countries adopt recruitment processes aimed at ensuring that audit staff have above-average knowledge and skills and adequate professional experience and that they undertake professional development.

Staffing and budgetary resource constraints and a lack of opportunity for upgrading staff skills through ongoing professional development were cited as problems in Brazil, Costa Rica, Dominican Republic, Honduras, Jamaica, and Paraguay. None of the CFAAs indicated that the SAIs in the sample countries had developed risk-based audit programs to direct attention to critical areas. Instead, the SAIs continued to direct their audits toward the legality and regularity of financial transactions. Auditing oriented toward examining the performance, economy, efficiency, and effectiveness of public administration remains rare. In fact, only Brazil had a performance auditing framework in place. Because of these staffing and budgetary resource constraints, SAIs also find it difficult to complete the full scope of their audit responsibilities on time— a significant weakness as the usefulness of even a first-rate audit is diluted if it is not timely.

Yet another important area of concern of the Lima Declaration is that the law should require auditees to comment on SAI findings within a specified period of time and to indicate the measures taken in response to those findings.[23] To the extent that SAI findings are not constitutionally delivered as enforceable judgments, the SAI should be empowered to require that action be taken and responsibility be accepted for any adverse findings. In general, none of the CFAAs indicated that SAIs had the authority to apply sanctions to address identified deficiencies, although the Brazil and Chile CFAAs indicated that agencies responded to audit findings. Some CFAAs explicitly mentioned that the SAI did not have authority to follow up on its findings (Dominican Republic, Paraguay), and others stated that the SAIs lacked an enforcement mechanism (Guatemala, Jamaica). Because of the SAIs' lack of enforcement power, government institutions and public officials have few concerns about the consequences of an SAI audit. Thus the external audit is less than effective as a tool to hold officials accountable for their management of public resources.

A final area of concern of the Lima Declaration is that SAIs be empowered to audit all public operations regardless of whether and how they are reflected in the national budget. In addition, to the extent that government exerts significant influence over state-owned enterprises, such organizations should be audited by the SAI. As mentioned earlier, some countries in the sample use off-budget entities or other nontransparent budgetary mechanisms to allocate state resources out of the public's view. Chile ensures that those agencies are audited and makes public summary financial information about those agencies. In Brazil, the SAI is responsible for auditing all 1,100 agencies of the government, but it lacks the staff to fulfill this obligation. In the Dominican Republic, Guatemala, Honduras, and Paraguay, SAIs are empowered to audit state-owned enterprises and other off-budget agencies, but they lack the capacity to fulfill that responsibility.

### Legislative Oversight

All CFAAs reported that the legislature of each country in the sample reviewed and debated the proposed budget. Because each legislature is mostly controlled by the president's political party and party loyalty is adhered to strictly, there is little incentive for legislators to deviate from the party line during the budget debate.[24] Moreover, legislators have limited access to technical expertise, and so their ability to debate technical issues of budget content is limited.

Except for Jamaica, none of the countries studied perform adequate legislative oversight of public spending. In most countries, there is little incentive to focus on past spending; legislators from the president's party have limited interest in finding fault with the government, and opposition legislators lack incentives to debate a technically arcane report. As a result, the legislature usually conducts a perfunctory vote to accept the SAI's annual report. And, except for Jamaica, few detailed questions are asked about the contents of the annual report, and there is no follow-up to correct any deficiencies identified in it.

### Level 3 Summary

Table 2.3 provides an assessment of the state of the main elements of efficient and effective delivery of public sector services and programs for each country sampled. When a country had weaknesses in aggregate fiscal discipline and strategic resource allocation, it also was very likely

**Table 2.3    Level 3: Efficient and Effective Delivery of Services and Programs**

| Issue | Brazil | Chile | Colombia | Costa Rica | Dom. Rep. | Guatemala | Honduras | Jamaica | Panama | Paraguay |
|---|---|---|---|---|---|---|---|---|---|---|
| Predictability of funding | 2 | 1 | 3 | 2 | 3 | 3 | 3 | 3 | 2 | 3 |
| Managing for results | 2 | 1 | 3 | 3 | 3 | 3 | 3 | 3 | 2 | 3 |
| Internal controls | 3 | 1 | 3 | 2 | 3 | 3 | 3 | 3 | 3 | 3 |
| Internal audit | 3 | 1 | 3 | 3 | 3 | 3 | 3 | 3 | 3 | 3 |
| External oversight | 2 | 2 | 3 | 3 | 3 | 3 | 3 | 3 | 3 | 3 |
| Legislative oversight | 3 | 2 | 3 | 3 | 3 | 3 | 3 | 1 | 3 | 3 |

*Note:* 1 = adequate or above; 2 = could benefit from strengthening; 3 = weak; empty cell = nothing reported in CFAA. These ratings reflect a qualitative judgment based on the subjective diagnosis presented in the CFAAs.

to exhibit weaknesses in the efficient and effective delivery of services and programs.

Predictability of funding depends on having reliable hard budget constraints so that the treasury can release cash to individual entities to meet the costs of their policies and programs as needed. Chile focuses explicitly on the predictability of funding and achieves it to a high degree. Brazil's revenue forecasts tend to be overly optimistic, leading to frequent midyear corrections. Costa Rica and Panama have good systems for providing funds to agencies, but excessive ex ante controls constrain the timeliness of actual cash releases. Although Colombia and Jamaica employ good cash management systems, predictability of funding is limited by constraints on the availability of cash.

An area of consistent weakness across the region is managerial accountability for implementing the government's strategic priorities. Of the countries reviewed, only Chile, as described earlier, manages effectively for results. The other countries face challenges in moving to a results-focused culture.

First among these challenges are inadequate management information systems. Brazil, Chile, Colombia, Costa Rica, and Panama regularly produce monitoring indicators to enable senior government managers to track their results, but public sector managers generally do not use these information resources effectively. Because Brazil, Chile, Costa Rica, and Panama use programmatic budgetary classifications, they can track whether funds have been spent for their intended purposes, but generally only at the national level. Brazil, Chile, and Costa Rica have integrated their investments and recurrent budgets, but the other countries have difficulty evaluating the long-term implications of capital expenditures for their recurrent operations because of disaggregated budgets.

A second challenge is weak internal control and internal audit frameworks. Of all the countries sampled, only in Chile do public sector managers use the results of internal audits as informative managerial feedback. Costa Rica has also developed a blueprint that meets internationally recognized standards in this area.

A third challenge is that independent oversight arrangements have yet to develop a level of robustness to support a framework that fully devolves responsibility and therefore accountability for the implementation of government programs. The SAI in Chile is effective, and the SAI in Brazil is improving. Yet neither country issues auditors' opinions on the government's consolidated financial statements in a format that conforms to internationally recognized standards. Legislatures in the region are "typically characterized by operational, administrative, and resource problems that limit the fulfillment of their legislative, representative and oversight responsibilities" (Santiso 2004). Finally, as described earlier, civil society is still unable to play a full role because of inadequacies in the legal framework or because of lack of technical knowledge on the subject of public finances.

As stated at the beginning of this chapter, a prerequisite for attaining quality in the use of public resources is that a country successfully implement programs to make progress at all three levels described in the chapter, and that it address deficiencies at all levels simultaneously in order not to undermine progress in any one level. The example of Brazil, overall the second best performer in the countries reviewed, is illustrative.

Brazil has a reasonably robust PFM legal framework that incorporates a widely replicated fiscal responsibility law. It adopts a comprehensive budget that is compiled through a participatory process that includes the sectoral agencies and civil society. And it incorporates a medium-term planning framework and has a nationally integrated financial management system that, though aging, is able to capture budget execution information on a timely and accurate basis. Finally, despite resource constraints, Brazil's supreme audit institution is one of the strongest in the region, making steady progress in adopting international good practices such as performance auditing techniques. In other words, Brazil is making progress at all three levels.

And yet Brazil still faces challenges adopting a hard budget constraint (level 1) because of the extent to which revenue forecasts are adjusted upward during legislative consideration of the budget. Moreover, although the government articulates its strategic priorities in its multiyear framework (level 2), these priorities are undermined by the widespread use of constitutionally mandated earmarks. These two factors affect the availability of predictable funding (level 3) for the implementation of approved government programs. Midyear cash rationing is the norm. Ultimately, the effect is to constrain the government from achieving quality in the use of expenditures. For example, although the percentage of GDP spent on education is close to the OECD average, Brazil fares poorly in the OECD's PISA measurement of student performance in comparison with countries with similar spending on education (OECD 2005).[25]

## Notes

1. The most prominent was the Enron bankruptcy and the collapse of its pension fund in 2001.

2. Under the Brady Bond scheme, commercial banks accepted reduced debt values in exchange for guarantees of the refinanced debt by international agencies.

3. See http://www.intosai.org.

4. The other 11 are data dissemination, fiscal transparency, transparency in monetary and financial policies, banking supervision, securities market regulation, insurance supervision, payments and settlements, anti-money laundering, corporate governance, insolvency, and creditor rights.

5. These are Argentina, Brazil, Chile, Colombia, Dominican Republic, Ecuador, El Salvador, Guatemala, Haiti, Honduras, Jamaica, Mexico, Paraguay, Peru, Uruguay, and countries of the Organization of Eastern Caribbean States.

6. The historical perspective is drawn from Pendle (1990).

7. Information on the Westminster model can be found, for example, in U.K. Department for International Development 2004. "Characteristics of Different External Audit Models." Policy Division Information Series Briefing, Ref. no. PD Info 021.London.

8. As an example, the El Salvador ROSC A&A review included a detailed explanation of how the country decided to adopt the 2003 version of the IFRS as its standard, even though a major redesign of IFRS was expected in 2004. The country did not update its standard after issuance of the 2004 version of IFRS.

9. According to the handbook "IFRSs in Your Pocket 2007: An IAS Plus Guide" (Deloitte 2007), comprehensive changes were made to 5 of IFRS principles and 16 of IFRS standards in 2004. Subsequently, three principles and three standards were revised. There are also frequent changes in the interpretation of standards to reflect ongoing changes in financial instruments or transactions.

10. According to the Web site of the U.S. National Association of State Boards of Accountancy, the qualifications for becoming a certified public accountant (CPA) vary from state to state. They include: (1) a college education with

some coursework in accounting and ethics; (2) verifiable practical experience in accounting; (3) dedicated accounting education that meets International Education Standards; and (4) passage of an exam. A CPA wishing to maintain certification must keep current on changes in standards and the profession by taking continuing education courses that comply with International Education Standards.

11. In this case, "national jurisdiction" is used to describe an entity—such as Guernsey, Jersey, or Isle of Mann—which has its own country credit rating but is not a sovereign country.

12. The BRICS countries are Brazil, Russia, India, China, and South Africa.

13. CReCER is a forum for regional cooperation on issues of public financial management and corporate financial transparency co-organized by the World Bank, Inter-American Development Bank, and International Federation of Accountants.

14. For example, Argentina, Brazil, Colombia, and Mexico.

15. In Chile, the budgets of the regional authorities are included in the budget of the Ministry of the Interior.

16. These cash generators are the Itaipu Binacional, jointly owned with Brazil, which sells hydroelectricity to Brazil, and the Entidad Binacional Yacireta, jointly owned with Argentina, which sells hydroelectricity to Argentina.

17. According to OECD (2003), over 90 percent of Brazil's budget was estimated as being so earmarked.

18. In December 2005, the government of Guatemala issued the *Acuerdo Gubernativo* on General Norms for Access to Public Information, which sets out the obligation for government agencies to furnish information within 30 days. However, the *Acuerdo* does not establish any sanction for those agencies that do not comply.

19. Brazil, Chile, Colombia, Guatemala, and Panama had planning activities at the time of the CFAA. Costa Rica, Dominican Republic, and Honduras were developing multiyear planning processes to be introduced shortly after completion of the CFAAs.

20. In principle, capital and recurrent budgets could be prepared separately, which has the advantage of enabling proposed expenditures to be evaluated by appropriately specialized staff. However, communications between the two groups must be excellent, so that the impacts of investments on recurrent expenditures are fully taken into account.

21. The systems in Costa Rica, Guatemala, and Panama are appropriate and up-to-date. Similarly, Paraguay's accounting system was well designed, although it covers only the central administration, which makes up about 50 percent of the government. Brazil and Chile currently use old accounting systems that badly need upgrading. Those systems were state-of-the-art when they

were developed in the late 1980s and early 1990s. However, they are now overloaded, and their architecture lacks the capacity to change or to accept additions to the system. Jamaica's accounting system is also in serious need of upgrading because it relies on a combination of independently developed legacy components. Since their assessments, the Dominican Republic and Honduras have upgraded their accounting systems.

22. These units usually reside within a ministry, department or agency (MDA). They report either to the MDA or to a centralized internal audit coordinator within the ministry of finance or the office of the presidency.

23. The declaration presumes that the SAIs will complete individual entity audits on time. Virtually all SAIs have backlogs of incomplete or delayed audits. This problem is explicitly mentioned in the CFAAs for the Dominican Republic, Honduras, and Paraguay. The Colombia CFAA indicated that the audits of central government entities were timely, but that audits for subnational government units were late. The Colombia CFAA also indicated that the legislature refused to vote on the SAI's annual report because of inaccuracies.

24. In 8 of the 10 countries studied for this book, the president's party has a majority in the legislature.

25. The Programme for International Student Assessment (PISA) is an internationally standardized triennial assessment administered to 15-year-olds that seeks to measure scholastic performance.

# CHAPTER 3

# Findings from the Country Procurement Assessment Reports

This chapter sets out the main findings from the review of the Country Procurement Assessment Reports. As noted earlier in this report, OECD has developed and is currently testing a Methodology for Assessment of National Procurement Systems. Under the OECD framework, baseline indicators seek to benchmark procurement systems against international standards along four dimensions: (1) legal and regulatory framework; (2) institutional architecture; (3) operations management; and (4) independent oversight. Because this tool provides a framework that is increasingly widely recognized, the presentation of the findings from this review is closely aligned with these four dimensions.

The following sections set out an analytical discussion of procurement in the LAC region. The first section summarizes global developments over the last 20 years in procurement. The section that follows summarizes the status of procurement in the LAC region, thereby enabling a comparison of progress within the region and global trends. The final four sections are devoted to an analysis of how the LAC countries sampled have addressed the four dimensions just listed. Each section concludes with a table setting out the authors' judgment of country performance on each dimension.

## Recent Global Developments in Procurement

Public procurement is one of the fastest-changing government functions. Over the last 15 years, procurement has moved from an administrative function to a strategic responsibility that plays a critical role in public expenditure management, quality of governance, promotion of economic development, and commercial integration. The pace and progress of this evolution have, however, been uneven, and in many developing economies vestiges of the concept of procurement as a process function remain. In addition, in most countries procurement has not been fully integrated and aligned with the strategic vision and objectives of the government, thereby becoming an obstacle to, instead of a support for, meeting those objectives.

Until the early 1990s, the procurement function was typically confined to the application of rules for the government purchase of goods, services, and civil works. Procurement units were housed in individual ministries, and individual government agencies worked in isolation, with responsibilities limited to processing purchase orders or administering competitive bids. These procurement units delivered contract award recommendations for approval by senior officials and subsequent processing by the legal or financial units in the organization. They were generally understaffed, with officers who had no formal education in the subject. The function itself was regarded as a backroom activity that received little or episodic attention only when a procurement scandal or mishap emerged.

The modern concept of procurement is that of an essential support to good public sector performance and to achievement of the country's economic and social goals—in other words, it is an integral part of public expenditure management and is moving from being a mere processing task to a management and knowledge-based activity that supports good governance and enhanced accountability.

The procurement profession is being deeply affected by this evolution. At the operational level, procurement officers are less likely to be the administrators of an activity requiring mere knowledge and application of rules. Instead, they now increasingly need to be managers of a process requiring an array of skills, guided by ethical and accountability principles. The old procurement bureaucrat is gradually being replaced by a well-trained contract or logistics manager whose job is not only to apply the rules but also to operate within a sophisticated market of ever-increasing commercial and technological complexity. At the policy level, decision makers are now more aware of the potential impact that government procurement has on the efficient use of resources and service delivery, on conferring legitimacy and credibility on the government, and on supporting economic and social agendas.

Important developments in the early 1990s triggered this change in perspective. Some of these events forced governments to focus on procurement as they sought to adapt national systems to international trade agreements and to new business concerns. In addition, civil society's growing concerns about corruption and the greater demands for accountability and results put politicians on notice of the importance of procurement as a strategic government function. Several events or developments during this period served as important drivers in reforming procurement:

- In 1992 members of the European Community signed the Maastricht Treaty, creating the European Union. The multiplicity of national procurement systems was an impediment to free trade and forced governments to align their national systems. In the early 1990s, the European Commission issued a green paper on public purchasing to open the discussion on procurement with the private sector, the contracting bodies, and other stakeholders (Nielse and Treumer 2005). The result was a call for system simplification, modernization, and flexibility, which culminated in the procurement directives adopted in March 2004.

- In 1994 the Uruguay Round of the General Agreement on Trade and Tariffs (GATT) culminated in the signing in April 1994 of the Government Procurement Agreement (GPA) and the creation of the World Trade Organization in 1995. The GPA introduced a multilateral framework for government procurement that aimed to achieve greater liberalization and expansion of world trade.

- In 1994 the United Nations Commission on International Trade Law (UNCITRAL) published the Model Law on Procurement of Goods, Construction and Services. This law was "in response to the fact that in a number of countries the existing legislation governing procurement is inadequate and outdated," resulting in inefficiency and ineffectiveness in the procurement process, patterns of abuse, and the failure of governments to obtain value for money in the use of public funds (UNCITRAL 1999).

- In the mid-1990s, international development institutions shifted the focus of procurement due diligence from supervising borrower compliance with their policies and procedures to systemic analysis, risk assessment, and policy advice on how to improve national systems.

- Beginning in the early 1990s, technological innovation made available new tools for electronic procurement that revolutionized the ways in which governments could do business. These technologies made it possible to minimize or eliminate the interaction between procurement officials and bidders, reducing the opportunity for collusive practices. The new technology also permitted more efficient procurement methods (such as reverse auctions and catalog purchasing under framework contracts), wider competition, and the possibility of better monitoring of procurement and more informed planning.[1]

- In 2006 OECD began work on producing a standardized diagnostic tool to assess public procurement systems and their performance (OECD 2006). The long-term goal is that this tool will gradually evolve into an internationally accepted set of standards for good procurement that can be used by governments as a benchmarking and monitoring instrument.

## Status of Procurement in the Region

The present procurement systems in the LAC region were influenced by the cultural, legal, and political heritage of colonization. On the legal side, most systems originated in Napoleonic or Roman law (civil law) in which rules are codified and prescriptive and procedural formalities traditionally have been observed rather strictly. Under this system, in Latin America contracts between private citizens and the state become public contracts ruled by administrative law and subject to specific judicial control. This legal foundation generates the need for detailed regulation (Trepte 2004). By contrast, the Caribbean countries inherited the common law system in which contracts are subject to the jurisdiction of civil courts that treat the government like any other private party to a contract with no additional privileges applying. Despite this difference, a common concern of both subregions has been to ensure a full accounting of revenues and taxes, resulting in the development of a control focus in the management of public resources, including for procurement systems. However, this focus on control did not concern itself with issues of economy or efficiency.

Because of this prevailing control orientation, the preparation of laws and other legal norms has almost exclusively been left to the legal experts. Procurement experts, policymakers, and public sector economists have had little opportunity to promote the ideas of economic efficiency or commercial objectives as the drivers around which laws should be drafted. As a result, a culture has developed in which procedural formality overtakes the substance of good business decisions. In this context, it is not surprising that oversight systems also emphasize compliance with norms instead of stressing quality of outcomes and risk management. Finally, officials have developed a culture of risk aversion and excessive rigor in the application of norms that, in the long term, affects the willingness of firms to compete for business with the government. It has simply become too costly for them to do so, whether under Napoleonic or common law regimes.

Often the triggers for reforms to procurement regulation have been scandals, major corruption cases, or accumulated frustration with the system. In these circumstances, reforms have been carried out hastily by adding more controls and passing legislation to deal with the crisis—that is, equating improvements in transparency with the addition of more controls, but without a thorough analysis of the roots of the problem. With a few exceptions, such as Chile, reforms are not subjected to careful planning, political consensus, and forward-looking management. For example, recently in one country a failed bid (the only bidder, who offered twice the market price, was the winner of a large contract) triggered a flurry of press publicity and an urgency to reform the law. In its haste to assuage public concern and placate the media, the government drafted and submitted a new law to the legislature without allotting any time to thorough consultations with stakeholders. Meanwhile, the draft law did not address major issues identified in the CPAR, with the result that government arguably missed, in a bow to political expediency, a unique opportunity to modernize the system.

Business groups have been another important factor in shaping the present regulatory framework in the region. Professional and trade associations have pressed for reforms on two fronts. The first is the promotion of protectionist legislation—for example, through exclusion of foreign firms from national bidding or by granting price preferences or other special treatment to domestic firms. The second is simplification of norms and elimination of requisites and paperwork in bidding to reduce transaction costs. Businesses can exert more effective influence in the smaller countries, where the result may be their de facto capture of the system. Although progress has been limited in simplifying the system, the opposite is true in protecting local firms.

Because of the common factors that influenced their development, procurement systems across the region have common traits and face similar issues. However, the impact of existing deficiencies on the efficiency of public expenditures and on the behavior of markets depends to a large degree on the size of the economy.[2] This scale factor should be considered when assessing the severity of a particular issue and the priorities for reform. Thus although in Chile public procurement represents only 3.5 percent of the GDP, in Costa Rica it amounts to 20 percent and in Paraguay 38 percent. The average for the region is between 10 and 15 percent. In smaller countries where the state is the largest purchaser of goods and services, government procurement may become the de facto price setter for the goods and services it demands. And yet suppliers may find it easier to collude and artificially raise prices if competition is restricted to domestic firms and there are few of them, as is often the case.

Some factors, however, undermine the credibility and legitimacy of the government regardless of the market size. Examples are lack of transparency, frequent corruption scandals, and substandard products or construction. These factors always attract the interest of the media and the public and affect public trust in the government.

The rest of this chapter sets out in more detail the formidable challenges facing procurement reform across the region. When the situation is viewed in the context of the recent global developments described in the previous section, it is clear that to be successful, reforms in the region must be transformative. Such a transformation should aim to trigger an essential change in the culture of control and in the thinking of politicians, policymakers, procurement managers, and officers, because technological fixes alone will not work. Reform requires a set of explicit strategic objectives around which systems can be regulated and organized; it should not be initiated simply in reaction to a crisis. Fixing the regulatory framework or the institutions is necessary but not sufficient. Instead, the objectives of the procurement system should be synchronized with the government's broad strategic goals. See, for example, the situation described in box 3.1, which illustrates how a process and control approach can be transformed with increased efficiency in mind even in the context of a legalistic culture.

**Box 3.1**

## Panama: Multiple Procurement Regulatory Systems

Panama has three different sets of procurement regulations. All procurement carried out by government agencies was regulated until recently by Law 56 of 1995, an exceedingly formalistic and control-focused law, albeit vague and imprecise in critical aspects. Provisions of the law were fragmented, and interpretation was left mostly to the procurement agencies, resulting in inconsistent and unpredictable outcomes as well as the possibility of discrimination and arbitrariness. Procurement execution under this framework was generally perceived to be corrupt, inefficient, and unreliable.

Rather than undertake a fundamental reform of Law 56, Panamanians established two additional parallel frameworks. One is administered by the Panama Canal Authority and the other by the Social Security Administration (for procurement of drugs and other health sector goods). These two systems are generally perceived to be more efficient and reliable. Their regulations were developed with a strong focus on efficient and economic procurement rather than on compliance and control. That said, both systems include appropriate oversight provisions.

## Legal and Regulatory Framework

### Use of Rules to Influence the Market

As stated earlier, most regulatory systems in the region have developed with a strong emphasis on control; efficiency has taken a backseat to formality. Under this approach, laws and regulations aim to influence market behavior by means of specific prohibitions or mandatory requirements instead of incentives. For example, some countries mandate minimum domestic content in any offer (e.g., in Mexico all bids must incorporate domestic labor and materials equal to at least 50 percent of the total cost). If not, the proposal is rejected. This requirements hampers the ability of the bidder to source inputs freely and thus to submit the most economical proposal. Similarly, Mexican and Peruvian laws restrict participation in national competitive bids to domestic firms. Foreign firms cannot compete even if they are willing to do so under the rules of national competitive bidding.[3] An alternative policy approach might be to grant reasonable price preferences to domestic bids without constraining competition by prohibiting the participation of foreign firms.

### Approach to Procurement Regulation

Little or no analysis has been undertaken in the LAC region of the impact of regulation on efficiency. Regulations are often based on models from other countries (mostly continental Europe) or on the multilateral banks' policies on procurement. Or, as indicated earlier, rules are introduced to address weaknesses revealed by individual cases of corruption or scandals, or under pressure from business or interest groups. There is, however, little evidence that the adoption of a particular regulation is subject to systematic cost-benefit and equity analyses. For example, no systematic cost-benefit analysis is undertaken of the impact that domestic provider protections may have in the form of higher prices, technological obsolescence, or industry inefficiencies. In some LAC countries, large firms are already capable of competing successfully in the international market without any protection, whereas, particularly in small countries, indiscriminate local industry protection might end up fostering oligopolistic conditions and enabling a corrupt environment.

### Multiplicity of Regulations

The prevailing institutional arrangement for administering procurement in the region is centralized legislation and decentralized management by individual government agencies and ministries.[4] Regulation generally consists of a national procurement law (some countries have separate laws for goods, civil works, and services) and an associated regulatory decree. Detailed regulations and procedures are generally left to each agency. In countries with federal arrangements (Argentina, Brazil, Mexico), the states or provinces also have their own laws and regulations. Furthermore, most countries have special procurement regulations in place for government-owned enterprises such as oil industries or utilities (e.g., PETROECUADOR in Ecuador and some major public utilities in Colombia) or exclusions from the law such as the army in most countries. Other sets of special regulations are applied to autonomous corporations, in designated regional or national jurisdictions and for specific purposes.[5] In some LAC countries, as much as 50 percent of the total procurement is regulated under special regimes. Most of these special regimes were necessary because the existing national procurement laws lacked the required speed and flexibility. For example, PETROECUADOR procurement managers view the national law as outdated and inadequate to meet their business needs—needs that are more akin to those of the private sector. Politically, it has been easier to develop new, tailor-made systems for autonomous agencies than to reform outdated national laws.

The multiplicity of procurement regimes and the diversity of detailed regulations at the agency level have a direct impact on costs because suppliers tend to specialize in bidding for contracts with one or a few government agencies, thereby fragmenting the market and reducing competition. At times, this situation creates a "club mentality" that can lead to collusion and other abuses. For example, in Costa Rica contractors indicated that it is easier for them to specialize in bidding for work at a single or a few agencies, the rules of which they know well. Besides limiting competition, such a system produces a situation in which the aggregate transaction costs to the government and the public of managing multiple regulatory systems can be significant. The costs to the private sector of preparing documentation to meet the plethora of requirements by the different agencies are also significant. Contractors and consultants interviewed in Chile told how bidding for government contracts was at least twice as expensive as bidding for similar projects in the private sector because of the greater number of government requirements and time involved.

This proliferation of regulations is a formidable barrier to the advancement of international good practice based on equal access and treatment. It also complicates negotiation of free trade agreements in which procurement harmonization is invariably an important item on the agenda. Moreover, the existence of multiple regulatory regimes increases the legal risks for those doing business with the government. One important reason is that the lack of a unique regulatory function results in each agency developing its own interpretation of the law and jurisprudence (Costa Rica). Such an environment fosters arbitrariness and abuse. This issue is particularly critical in a region traditionally averse to arbitration or other forms of alternative dispute resolution (ADR).[6] Court practice and proceedings, even for relatively simple disputes, are widely considered to be unreliable, unpredictable, costly, and slow—a situation that worsens when disputes are settled by provincial or state courts in federal regimes. Bidders therefore factor this risk into their prices or are discouraged from participating.

### Systems Overburdened with Process

Excessive procedural formality characterizes the administration of procurement across the LAC region. When issues emerge because of deficiencies in the system, governments add regulations and controls piecemeal to existing ones, creating a package of norms that is, at times, contradictory and adds cost without adding value. Countries therefore need to reduce and streamline the accumulation of rules to enhance transparency and save processing time. Excessive process also fosters an environment in which "facilitation payments" to expedite decisions are common, encourages the fractioning of contracts (i.e., dividing large purchases into small packages) or leads to pleas of "exceptional circumstances" to circumvent the competitive process. The CPARs for Costa Rica and Brazil cited fractioning as a problem. In Brazil, the federal government also recognized that 50 percent or more of federal public procurement took place through noncompetitive methods, mainly in order to avoid the time-consuming bidding process.

In an effort to circumvent their own laws, many countries and agencies resort to using UN agencies, such as the United Nations Development Programme (UNDP) and United Nations Office for Project Services, as procurement agents. Brazil, Colombia, Guatemala, and Honduras, among others, make extensive use of these agencies not only for emergencies but also for normal operations. The pressure of having to spend money in a short time before the end of the fiscal year also fuels use of these agencies. Even though these arrangements may render short-term benefits, in the long term they remove pressure to reform the system and add cost to the procurement process. And yet there is no evidence of a formal exit strategy from the use of such agencies. Box 3.2 illustrates how excessive process affected procurement operations in Brazil and Panama, even with the use of UNDP in Panama.

### Excessive or Scant High-Level Regulation

The rigid regulatory frameworks in place in many countries do not permit rapid adaptation to fast-changing market conditions and new procurement techniques. In particular, high-level regulatory instruments incorporate excessive detail that is more appropriately included in lower-level instruments such as directives, manuals, standard bidding documents, and contract forms (Mexico, Brazil[7]). Colombia has learned this lesson after an experience in which the legislature took four years to pass reforms to the procurement law, considerably delaying modernization of the system.

By contrast, in Guatemala, Honduras, and Jamaica the procurement laws are vague or have lacunae. In the absence of unambiguous responsibility for regulatory aspects, the oversight agencies typically fill the vacuum. For example, in Costa Rica the comptroller general regulates areas of ambiguity through instructions and case law and can overrule the agencies' interpretation of law. Even in countries that have recently reformed

**Box 3.2**

## Panama and Brazil: The Impact of an Excessive Procurement Process

In Panama, the assessment of the line ministries provided some insight into the internal bottlenecks that contribute to delays and inefficiencies. For example, in the Ministry of Education contracting requires 20 administrative processes divided into 84 steps, of which all but 1 process and 2 steps are internal requirements of the ministry. The average time for a simple shopping process is six months. In the Ministry of Health, contracting requires 18 administrative processes divided into 69 steps, of which all but 1 process and 2 steps are internal requirements of the ministry. Typically, the Ministry of Public Works takes 246 days to complete a process under Law 56 and 180 days to process a project utilizing UNDP as the financial agent. Even within this simplified context, the ministry must complete 38 steps before allowing a contractor to mobilize.

In Brazil, the procurement law passed in 1993 gives more weight to compliance with procedural aspects rather than to the substance of procurement. This emphasis is a source of frequent and protracted disputes, which often end up in court. Consequently, public agencies have a strong incentive to resort to Article 24 of the law, which sets out 24 exceptions to compliance with competitive procedures. To address the problem, the government has invested in modern infrastructure and systems, such as the reverse auction (*pregão*) which provides a rapid and simple procurement process for off-the-shelf items and uncomplicated services, aiming at avoiding direct purchases. Over the period 2001–2002, the use of *pregão* reduced by 20 percent the number of contracts awarded through noncompetitive methods.

their regulatory systems, insufficient thought was given to what should be included in the law (the most difficult to amend) or in the regulations supporting the law (easier to reform) or in the administrative or operational instructions or documents (easiest to change).

Table 3.1 sets out the legal and regulatory issues most frequently mentioned in the sample CPARs as still needing attention across the region and the relative severity of such issues in each country. Across all these countries, the scope for improvement in the basic legal and regulatory environment is enormous.

**Table 3.1    Procurement Legal and Regulatory Framework**

| Issue | Brazil | Chile | Colombia | Costa Rica | Dom. Rep. | Guatemala | Honduras | Jamaica | Panama | Paraguay |
|---|---|---|---|---|---|---|---|---|---|---|
| Quality of regulatory system | 2 | 2 | 2 | 2 | 3 | 3 | 3 | 2 | 2 | 1 |
| Regulatory framework | 3 | 3 | 3 | 3 | | 3 | | | 3 | |
| Procurement manuals and instructions | 3 | 2 | 3 | 3 | 3 | 3 | 3 | 2 | | 2 |
| Standard bidding documents | 3 | 3 | 3 | 3 | 3 | 3 | 3 | 3 | 3 | 2 |
| Framework for selection of consultants | | 2 | 3 | 3 | | 3 | | | 2 | |
| Year present procurement law enacted (Most laws have been amended since their initial enactment.) | 1993, 2002 | 2004 | 1993 | 1996 | 2006 | 1992 | 2001 | NA | 2006 | 2003 |

Note: 1 = adequate or above; 2 = could benefit from strengthening; 3 = weak; empty cell = nothing reported in CPAR; NA = not applicable. These ratings reflect a qualitative judgment based on the subjective diagnosis presented in the CPARs.

## Institutional Architecture

### Unifying Vision and Interagency Coordination

In most of the LAC countries reviewed, no single agency is designated to take the lead on procurement policy formulation and coordination. The main protagonists are normally the ministries of finance and planning, the ministries of public works, and the large energy utilities. The comptroller's office or equivalent also has an important role in shaping the system.

The CPARs did not report the existence in any country (perhaps with the exception of Chile) of any formal and substantive interagency coordination mechanism. Such a mechanism could serve as a forum for reconciling regulations and ensuring that they are consistent with the government's policy objectives and development plans. Often agencies have different or even divergent objectives without an institutional mechanism for alignment and coordination between them and overall government objectives and strategy. For example, although the ministry of finance may be interested in promoting competition to obtain lower prices, the ministry of industry and commerce may be issuing instructions limiting foreign firms' participation in bidding for government contracts, which would raise prices. The frequent turf battles for dominance in the procurement arena also hampers progress toward better systems. For example, in Colombia the launch of procurement reform was delayed largely because of the lack of agreement among three leading government agencies. Although there have been proposals to create public procurement councils at the cabinet level to ensure such coordination, none currently exists.

## System Management

In an effort to mitigate the impact of the proliferation of regulations and procedures, several countries have created organizations or units to oversee the performance of procurement operations, analyze markets and develop procurement strategies, issue regulations and procedures, formulate policies, provide training, and resolve precontractual disputes. Examples of these types of agencies are CONSUCODE (Concejo Superior de Contrataciones del Estado) in Peru, the Secretariat of Public Administration (Secretaría de la Función Pública) in Mexico, the DGCP (Dirección General de Contrataciones Públicas) in Paraguay, and the National Contracts Commission in Jamaica. However, most of these agencies do not have the political influence to perform their duties, and many are struggling to assert their mandates (see box 3.3).

---

**Box 3.3**

### Costa Rica: The Struggle of a Procurement Regulatory Body

According to the stipulations of Costa Rica's Law No. 8131, the General Office for the Administration of Administrative Goods and Services (DGABCA) within the Ministry of Finance is the oversight body for the procurement of goods. DGABCA exercises a normative role (i.e., guidelines, regulations, policies, and information systems). It also supervises the central government agencies, which since 2002 have been responsible for their own institutional procurement units. Municipalities have their own procurement units as well.

The most significant limitation that DGABCA faces is the lack of people and budget to fulfill its current role. Moreover, the procurement law excludes from its remit the autonomous institutions that account for 92 percent of the budget allocated for public procurement. DGABCA's activities have thus concentrated primarily on the development of COMPRARED, an electronic procurement network that has been implemented only in the central government to date.

In view of this situation, the CPAR recommends: "Although DGABCA's actions are moving in the right direction, it would be a good idea to establish a consulting supervisory body for the entire public sector to provide leadership and oversee the strategic vision of the contracting system. In order to do this, it will be necessary to pass legal reforms that will allow the Head Office to fulfill this objective."

### Electronic Procurement

Progress in developing electronic procurement platforms has been encouraging. Most countries see e-procurement as a potential driver of modernization, greater transparency, and efficiency. Brazil, Chile, and Mexico have pioneered the use of e-procurement (see box 3.4). Colombia, Panama, and Paraguay have completed the first phase of system enhancements that provide information on business opportunities and regulations. They are starting a second phase to establish transactional capabilities and links to budget execution systems. Development of e-procurement in Guatemala is well advanced, but at the time of the

---

**Box 3.4**

## Chile: Promoting Participation in Electronic Procurement

Lack of participation by purchasing agencies and suppliers because of inadequate knowledge and technical support was one of the main reasons for failure of the initial phase of CHILECOMPRA, the most advanced e-procurement system in the region today. Therefore, a key element of Chile's Public Procurement Program Strategic Plan (PPSSP) is the development and implementation of long-term programs of dissemination and technical assistance for users and suppliers and, in particular, for regional offices and municipalities. Because procurement modernization is expected to produce considerable savings, government agencies are required to cover, out of their own resources, technical assistance and training expenses. This requirement apparently has not been a major problem for national agencies, but it will likely be a constraint for small municipalities.

Technical assistance includes the following major activities: (1) intensive dissemination and training of state agencies through the Program of Excellence in Procurement Management (Programa de Excelencia en Gestión de Abastecimiento) linked to the Ministry of Finance's Program of Management Improvement (Program de Mejoramiento de Gestión); (2) human resource development through on-the-job and formal training of staff, including the establishment of university courses on procurement management; and (3) technical support to user agencies on specific issues related to the operation of CHILECOMPRA. Support to suppliers focuses on (1) establishment of a National Registry of Suppliers; (2) dissemination of information on the benefits of CHILECOMPRA; (3) support to small and medium enterprises; and (4) dissemination of national and international business opportunities.

CPAR it remained underused. The Dominican Republic, Honduras, and Jamaica had yet to develop the basic strategies to establish e-procurement.

Notwithstanding progress on technical developments in e-procurement, several factors have impeded use of its full potential. Outdated legislation originally developed for paper-based methods has hampered progress in Mexico and Peru. In most countries, larger government agencies prefer to maintain their own e-procurement systems (often seen as symbols of prestige and technical sophistication) because the government cannot compel them to use a single official site. Persuading those agencies to switch to a new system that is unfamiliar to them is a major obstacle to unification. In Guatemala and Chile, it has been difficult to integrate municipalities into the central e-procurement system because it would violate decentralization and autonomy principles. In Paraguay, the lack of Internet connectivity and its high costs (three times as much as in neighboring countries) have forced the General Directorate of Public Contracting to install Internet booths in municipalities and other public offices to facilitate access to the system. Cultural prejudice has also impeded the widespread use of e-procurement—many bidders still do not trust the security levels of electronic systems and prefer paper-based transactions. As a result, governments have to continue operating parallel electronic and paper bidding processes.

In addition to its high cost, the proliferation of e-procurement sites generates other problems. First, the standards for the maintenance of critical information such as regulatory information may vary between systems. Ideally, only one official site should be designated to provide information critical to suppliers, contractors, and the public in order to limit the distribution of inconsistent information and the resulting errors in bids. Second, only one site should accurately capture the whole procurement cycle and provide all procurement information for analytical, investigative, and output monitoring purposes. However, the multiplicity of e-systems has prevented efforts to achieve this ideal. Third, integration of the procurement and budget systems is becoming more difficult because of the need to create appropriate interfaces between each individual e-system and the budget system. In some countries, agencies that have individual systems are obliged to enter the information on their transactions in the budget execution systems manually, with the attendant higher cost and likelihood of errors.

Table 3.2 sets out the procurement institutional architecture issues most frequently mentioned in the sample CPARs as being still in need of attention across the region and the relative severity of such issues. Chile

**Table 3.2    Procurement Institutional Architecture**

| Issue | Brazil | Chile | Colombia | Costa Rica | Dom. Rep. | Guatemala | Honduras | Jamaica | Panama | Paraguay |
|---|---|---|---|---|---|---|---|---|---|---|
| Political commitment for reforms | 2 | 1 | 2 | 3 | 3 | 2 | 3 | 3 | 1 | |
| Comprehensive public procurement vision, strategy, and plan | 2 | 1 | 2 | 3 | 3 | 3 | 3 | 3 | 2 | 2 |
| Adequate procurement professionals | 3 | 2 | 3 | 2 | | 3 | 3 | 3 | 3 | 3 |
| Accreditation systems and continuing professional development programs | 3 | 2 | 3 | 3 | 3 | 3 | 3 | 3 | 3 | 2 |
| Defined career paths and merit-based promotions | 3 | 3 | 3 | 3 | | 3 | 3 | 2 | 3 | 3 |
| Designated regulatory body | 3 | 1 | 2 | 2 | | 2 | | 2 | 2 | 1 |
| Institutional coordination of procurement policies | 1 | 1 | 2 | 3 | | 2 | | 3 | 2 | 1 |
| Status of development of e-procurement | 2 | 2 | 3 | 3 | 3 | 2 | 3 | 3 | 3 | 2 |

*Note:* 1 = adequate or above; 2 = could benefit from strengthening; 3 = weak; empty cell = nothing reported in CPAR. These ratings reflect a qualitative judgment based on the subjective diagnosis presented in the CPARs.

is far ahead of the other countries. Brazil and Paraguay have modernized some elements of their procurement architecture, but across the board there is room for tremendous gains.

## Operations Management

### Budget Planning and Execution

Throughout the LAC region, there is generally poor coordination between procurement planning and implementation, on one hand, and budget planning and execution, on the other. This observation is important because such integration would facilitate monitoring the use of resources and minimize the risk of bribery to expedite payments. Aggregate multiyear plans did not necessarily mirror the multiyear plans of individual government agencies. A similar misalignment occurred between annual national budgets and agencies' operating and procurement plans. Uncertainty and frequent changes of government procurement plans affect private sector preparedness to satisfy public sector demands, particularly for goods that must be manufactured to order and require advance production plant scheduling. Private sector firms accordingly factor delays or unpredictability of payments into higher prices.

## Dispute Resolution

Twenty-three countries in the LAC region adhere to the United Nations Convention on the Recognition and Enforcement of Foreign Arbitral Awards (1958), under which countries agree to enforce arbitrated awards issued abroad. Nineteen countries ratified the Inter-American Convention on International Commercial Arbitration (1975). Meanwhile, precontractual and contractual dispute resolution is an area in which much work remains to be done. However as mentioned earlier, the region is generally reluctant to resolve conflicts outside the courts. Because the region's courts are slow and bureaucratic and because some are vulnerable to corruption, the absence of well-regulated and effective alternate dispute resolution mechanisms discourages competition and increases prices. This deficiency also creates fertile grounds for abuse and arbitrariness and detracts from governments' credibility and legitimacy. Chile, Mexico, Panama, Paraguay, and Peru have specialized mechanisms to address precontractual disputes, but in most countries the contracting agency is the only place to appeal outside the tribunals. There is typically no general regulation on the procedures, the terms for resolution, or the obligation to follow up and post decisions publicly. A similar situation characterizes contractual disputes because of the reluctance of the governments to accept arbitration or similar ADR provisions as the first option instead of the courts.

## Availability of Information

Few procurement systems in the countries sampled captured reliable, relevant information on procurement operations, performance, and outcomes. Comprehensive information is fundamental for assessing a procurement system's aggregate performance, verifying compliance with the law, benchmarking prices, analyzing market trends, and developing supply chain management strategies. At the same time, regular publication of reports that contain relevant, easily understood information is essential to enhancing civil society participation. When assessed, most systems did not have a central repository of information that was easily accessible by those with a legitimate interest (e.g., planners, comptrollers, or civil society). Information tended to be dispersed across government agencies, and its integrity and reliability were uneven. Because of this lack of robust information, civil society oversight of procurement is often limited to a few individual transactions instead of entire programs.

### Human Resources

Traditionally, the procurement function in the LAC region has been weaker than other public service functions. Agency managers have neglected the function because they give it little strategic value. In general, the heads of procurement units and staff do not have the expertise and formal training required to perform the function. Learning has been on the job, perpetuating the vices and practices of the past and depriving agencies of the chance to modernize. Furthermore, in almost all countries there is no procurement career stream. Selection and promotion are rarely competitive or merit-based; instead, they tend to be based on political, social, or professional connections. The one emerging exception to this tendency is the cadre of technical staff working on the technological aspects of e-procurement—they are generally well trained. This situation is in sharp contrast to that in the private sector, where skill requirements for procurement professionals are high and where, recognizing its centrality to cost-efficiency, senior management pays close attention to the function by regularly monitoring procurement strategies and performance and meeting with chief procurement officers. In interviews conducted as part of the CPAR process, heads of procurement indicated that, absent a procurement scandal being reported in the media, they rarely met with senior government officials (vice ministers or ministers) to review procurement performance.

As noted earlier, procurement is evolving from an administrative task to a complex, knowledge-based function that covers the entire cycle of needs assessment, administration, contract implementation management, and asset disposal. Present public procurement thus requires well-trained professional managers of procurement operations who are capable of working in complex and sophisticated business environments. The shortage of skilled procurement professionals at the managerial and operational levels are a major hindrance to good procurement operations in the region. All CPARs report this shortage as a critical issue. The frequent turnover of staff (particularly in managerial positions) arising from changes in administration and political interventions exacerbates this problem.

### Decentralization

Most countries in the region have promoted administrative decentralization, including devolution of procurement responsibilities to subnational governments. This approach affords more direct participation of communities in projects, program design, and procurement oversight. At the same time, institutional weaknesses and lack of procurement skills deepen with decentralization, and many subnational entities cannot justify having a full-time procurement officer. Training programs, where they exist, focus on compliance with legal formalities, but not on how to purchase well. For example, in Peru CONSUCODE had an ambitious training program for local offices, but it was limited mostly to the regulatory aspects of procurement. Normally, there are no instructions or manuals, simple model contracts, or basic instructions for evaluation of small civil works proposals. Small communities and towns, usually in remote areas, exhibit the highest poverty indices. Compared with those in with larger communities and towns, their oversight mechanisms are weaker and more vulnerable to political pressure, leaving them open to misuse of resources through incompetent procurement, which, in view of already high poverty rates, has a significant opportunity cost for them. Thus decentralization requires stronger civil society participation, and yet there is no evidence of a concerted effort to organize and train communities accordingly.

Table 3.3 sets out the operations management issues most frequently mentioned in the sample CPARs as still needing attention across the region and the relative severity of such issues. Again, the table depicts the same situation on view in the other tables in this chapter: Chile and Paraguay are relatively successful in improving their operational performance, but the other countries are missing an opportunity.

## Independent Oversight

### Supreme Audit Institutions

In all countries reviewed, legislatures are responsible for the ultimate oversight of procurement operations through their review of the periodic (usually annual) audited reports submitted to them by the supreme audit institution. There is much consistency on issues affecting SAI oversight as reported in the CPARs. The most important of these, which are virtually identical to the more extensive discussion in the previous chapter, are the following:

- SAIs lacked technically skilled staff and were dependent on the executive for their budgets, including salaries, which potentially jeopardizes their independence.

**Table 3.3    Procurement Operations Management**

| Issue | Brazil | Chile | Colombia | Costa Rica | Dom. Rep. | Guatemala | Honduras | Jamaica | Panama | Paraguay |
|---|---|---|---|---|---|---|---|---|---|---|
| Procurement planning | | | 3 | 3 | | 3 | 3 | | 3 | 1 |
| Integration with budget and financial management system | | | 3 | | | 3 | | 3 | 3 | 2 |
| Information and monitoring systems | | 1 | 3 | 3 | | 3 | 3 | 3 | 3 | 1 |
| Consolidation of procurement across agencies | | 1 | 3 | 3 | | 3 | | 3 | 2 | 3 |
| Process and time required to process contracts | 2 | 3 | | | | 2 | | | 3 | 2 |
| Effectiveness and credible alternative dispute resolution | 3 | 3 | 3 | | | | | | | 1 |

*Note:* 1 = adequate or above; 2 = could benefit from strengthening; 3 = weak; empty cell = nothing reported in CPAR. These ratings reflect a qualitative judgment based on the subjective diagnosis presented in the CPARs.

- Risk identification, economy and efficiency, and the appropriate selection of procurement methods and results received no emphasis. Instead, the emphasis was on compliance with process and formal rules, which adds little or no value. And yet there were also some promising developments. In Chile and Brazil, the SAI was preparing risk maps to improve audit planning.
- There was a lack of interaction and communication with management and poor rectification of adverse audit findings.
- In Chile, Costa Rica, and Panama, the SAI was inappropriately involved in ex ante and concurrent review, amounting to co-management of the procurement process. In these countries, because of regulatory lacunae, the SAI was regulating procurement through its interventions and decisions.

### Civil Society Oversight

Civil society participation is increasingly recognized as a critical element of any balanced system of accountability. As such, it has a role in monitoring procurement operations, ensuring efficient delivery of public goods and services, and promoting demand for good governance. In most countries, there is awareness that the electoral process itself is an inadequate oversight mechanism for day-to-day resource management and for ensuring accountability in public procurement. Therefore, many civil society organizations are increasingly taking direct action, and most governments now recognize that CSO participation lends them legitimacy and credibility.

Nevertheless, the degree to which CSOs understand and are involved in public procurement is uneven across countries, and there seems to be a direct correlation between the weakness of the procurement function and the degree of involvement of the CSOs—that is, the weaker the system, the less involved CSOs are likely to be. For example, in the Dominican Republic, where the system was weak, over 5,000 CSOs could become an important force in generating demand for efficient and transparent procurement. However, no CSO has a primary focus on procurement.[8] By contrast, in Mexico a federal law to promote the activities of CSOs formalizes their participation, which takes many forms. Colombia has advanced legislation on the matter (box 3.5), but implementation is lagging. In Peru, civil society is active. Some groups are very sophisticated (box 3.6), but the perception is that they are weak and disorganized. As one person observed during the preparation

---

**Box 3.5**

## Colombia: A Legal Framework for Civil Society Participation

Colombia offers a progressive model of government promotion of civil society participation. In 2003 the country enacted modern legislation (Law no. 850) on the role, rights, and obligations of civil society oversight organizations (Veedurías Ciudadanas) and the scope and nature of their work. The law grants citizens the right to organize oversight bodies and sets out the obligation for public agencies and officials to cooperate with them and facilitate their work. The law also promotes the creation of networks of oversight organizations and an institutional network to support them (members are the attorney general, comptroller general, government ombudsman, and the Ministry of the Interior). The law assigns the training of the oversight organizations to the School of Public Administration. The performance evaluation of the program is the responsibility of the Administrative Department of the Funcion Publica. Progress in implementing the program has been slow, mostly because of a shortage of resources to finance the initial setup and administrative expenses of the oversight organizations. There are, however, encouraging signs that the system is gradually taking root across the country. One of the major risks of the program is capture by grassroots politicians for personal political gain.

**Box 3.6**

# Peru: How Civil Society Participates

The Peru CPAR team interviewed a cross section of civil society representatives: Camara de Comercio, MacroConsult, COMEXPERU, ProEtica, Transparencia, Ciudadanos Al Dia, Capital Humano y Social, Instituto de Defensa Legal. The following are examples of what they are doing:

- *Promoting good governance.* One CSO, Ciudadanos Al Dia (CAD), launched a competition to recognize good practices in government;
- *Monitoring procurement.* Various civil society organizations conduct social audits of public agencies at both the national and subnational levels;
- *Monitoring the "Special Fund" of illegally acquired funds.* This project, was set up to monitor the management and use of illegally amassed funds recovered by the state;
- *Conducting research, surveys, and risk maps.* CSOs conduct research that informs policy recommendations and conduct corruption surveys that seek to measure citizen perceptions;
- *Compiling databases.* ProEtica has gathered and posts on the Internet information on the compensation, declared assets, and experience of public officials for the regional government of Lambayeque;
- *Preparing proposals for reforms and offering recommendations to improve the system;*
- *Building demand for change.* Civil society works to alter the dialogue and demonstrate how corruption is robbery "against me." To do this, Peruvian CSOs regularly organize conferences that promote policy dialogue and bring together public officials with citizens and conduct a variety of campaigns to increase citizen and public official awareness;
- *Providing training.* CSOs provide training about the procurement law that complements a program that the U.S. Agency for International Development is supporting within CONSUCODE;
- *Undertaking comparative analysis.* The aim is to determine whether a particular agency or government has improved its purchasing of certain types of goods or whether the cost of providing services of similar quality is better in one location than in another and why;
- *Promoting strategic alliances between the private and public sectors;*
- *Designing and monitoring "integrity pacts."* Using a tool designed by Transparency International, CSOs have drafted integrity pacts aimed an increasing transparency and integrity in public and private sector institutions.

of the CPAR in 2004, "No NGO or coalition is powerful enough to do anything." Another mentioned that there were no legal or institutional incentives for the government to listen to civil society. That said, the media in Peru are particularly vocal, and stories of alleged corruption appear regularly. Thus, according to many other persons contacted, the government pays attention to civil society primarily via the press.

Despite the large number of respectable CSOs that could work on procurement across the LAC region, a lack of capacity hampers efforts to undertake basic social oversight activities outside the large cities because knowledge of procurement processes is weak. The subject is considered too technical, and there are few programs to train CSOs at the district or community level. Little work has been done to organize social oversight in villages, and members of such groups are often the target of organized intimidation. Unless capacity and safety can be improved for civilian oversight, it is difficult to imagine how effective oversight could be organized at the decentralized level of villages.

### Access to Information

To play their role effectively, CSOs must have the rights, tools, and skills to do so. Even though most countries constitutionally grant citizens the right to information, some governments still do not have detailed regulations implementing the right of citizens to access information on procurement. For example, at the time of the CPAR Guatemala had still not regulated public access to information, even though it is a constitutional right. This lack of regulation makes interpretation of this right arbitrary.[9] Therefore, there is no authoritative legal basis for requesting public officials to provide citizens with information. In general, the culture of disclosure does not exist in public agencies, and officials tend to use loopholes to avoid disclosure. Without a clear legal framework that requires government officials to provide information to the public or to respond to requests, monitoring by civil society becomes impossible.

Effective civil society oversight also requires that government agencies generate and widely disseminate reliable, relevant information on public procurement on a regular basis. Reports must be easily understood by citizens. Brazil, Chile, Mexico, Paraguay, and Peru post procurement information on their e-procurement Web sites, but often the public cannot interrogate the systems to produce tailor-made reports. Data mining and navigation are complicated, e-procurement only covers a fraction of the transactions, and the degree of technological literacy needed to access the

**Table 3.4    Independent Oversight of Procurement**

| Issue | Brazil | Chile | Colombia | Costa Rica | Dom. Rep. | Guatemala | Honduras | Jamaica | Panama | Paraguay |
|---|---|---|---|---|---|---|---|---|---|---|
| Ex post focus | 3 | | | 3 | | | | 3 | 3 | 2 |
| Effective internal controls | | | 2 | | | 2 | | 3 | 2 | 2 |
| Risk-based and value for money approaches | | | 2 | 3 | | | | 2 | 3 | 3 |
| Availability of procurement information. | | | 2 | 3 | 3 | 3 | 3 | 3 | 3 | |
| Capacity of civil society | | | 2 | 2 | | | 2 | | 1 | |
| Independent review of precontractual complaints | 3 | 1 | 3 | | | 3 | 3 | 3 | 3 | 1 |

*Note:* 1 = adequate or above; 2 = could benefit from strengthening; 3 = weak; empty cell = nothing reported in CPAR. These ratings reflect a qualitative judgment based on the subjective diagnosis presented in the CPARs.

information is beyond what exists in many of the countries. This issue is particularly relevant to procurement monitoring efforts in rural or remote communities.

Table 3.4 sets out the independent oversight issues most frequently mentioned in the sample CPARs as still needing attention across the region and the relative severity of such issues. Consistent with the findings in the previous chapter, most of the countries reviewed face important challenges in improving independent oversight of procurement functions.

## Notes

1. The terminology for new approaches to procurement is not fully settled. An *electronic reverse auction* is an online, real-time dynamic auction between the purchasing organization and suppliers who compete against each other to win the contract by submitting successively lower-priced or better-ranked bids over a scheduled period. A *framework agreement* between one or more contracting agencies and one or more suppliers or vendors establishes the terms (prices and the quantities envisaged) that will govern contracts to be awarded during a given period.

2. The case of Honduras is somewhat exceptional because international agencies such as the World Bank and the International Development Bank finance about 75 percent of public procurement, which is carried out under the policies and procedures required by these financiers.

3. These provisions may be indicative of system capture by domestic business groups, but in some cases such provisions work well and can be applied

transparently, such as allocation of market shares to the small and medium enterprises or specific disadvantaged groups.

4. In some countries in the English-speaking Caribbean (e.g., Guyana), a central tender board carries out procurement for the entire government.

5. At times, other organizations enjoy special procurement regimes created for a specific and finite purpose. One example is an agency associated with the reconstruction undertaken in response to the devastation caused by the El Niño weather phenomenon. Although the reconstruction was completed long ago, the agency remains responsible for tasks not clearly related to the original objective in order to take advantage of a more agile and up-to-date procurement regime that meets other government needs.

6. Many countries have adopted the Calvo Doctrine, formulated in the second half of the nineteenth century to protect them from intervention by foreign governments in legal disputes with their nationals. An extension of this doctrine precludes foreign firms from arbitrating disputes and requires that such disputes be submitted to local courts.

7. In Brazil, all instructions and guidance to public officials are required to be enshrined in law. Public officials cannot therefore be called to account for failure to take actions that are contained in, for example, departmental procedural guidelines but are not codified under law.

8. CSOs such as Paricipación Ciudadana, Fundación Institucionalidad y Justicia, and Fundación Solidaridad have produced important work on procurement and transparency, even though their focus is on broader governance and democracy issues.

9. In December 2005, the government issued the *Acuerdo Gubernativo* on General Norms for Access to Public Information that sets out the obligation for government agencies to furnish information within 30 days. However, the *Acuerdo* does not establish any sanction for those that do not comply.

# CHAPTER 4

# Revitalizing Reforms

Over the last two decades, many of the LAC countries embarked on a first wave of reforms designed to address technological constraints, achieve fiscal discipline, and improve the level of transparency in government operations. The starting point of these efforts was the adoption of automated management information systems for governments so that they could more easily compile, consolidate, and share information about budgets and spending; manage cash, revenues, and debt; and monitor compliance with government rules and procedures. Over the same period, there was also growing awareness of the importance of procurement as a strategic function. Governments accordingly looked to e-procurement solutions, updated legal and regulatory frameworks for procurement, and undertook related institutional reforms.

## Drivers and Results of Reforms

The drivers for this first wave of reforms stemmed from four main factors:

- *Entry of new administrations after extended periods of authoritarian rule.* Building on what can perhaps best be described as a "never again" consensus, several governments embarked on programs to increase accountability, effectiveness, and transparency. For example, in Panama an incoming administration inherited significant public debt, among the highest in the region, arising from off-budget transactions with unregistered contractors. Procurement reform was thus one of its first priorities. Other countries that fall in this category are Chile, Peru and, based on early indications, Paraguay.[1]

- *Search for debt relief.* Mexico's debt default of 1982 made clear the scope of global debt problems and kicked off various debt relief programs, such as the Baker and Brady Plans, throughout the late 1980s. These plans largely focused on the private sector. By the mid-1990s, it had become apparent that there were also significant numbers of highly indebted poor countries, giving rise to the Heavily Indebted Poor Countries (HIPC) Initiative, launched by the International Monetary Fund and World Bank, under which sovereign debt was forgiven or rescheduled. Although the majority of HIPC countries are in Sub-Saharan Africa, some countries in the LAC region also benefited. Thus, for example, when in 2003 the incoming administration in Honduras needed to address a series of pressing financial needs related to the country's strategic objective of reducing poverty, it sought debt relief under the HIPC program. However, it was required to put in place reforms, sound policies, and good governance that were supportive of pro-poor spending.

- *Demand for good governance.* Arguably, the most significant influence in increasing the demand for good governance arose with the establishment in 1993 of Transparency International, a global civil society organization. Its mission has been to raise awareness of the impact of corruption on the lives of citizens. Its establishment and the light it shone on mismanagement of government finances worldwide empowered civil society and media organizations in developing countries to begin to ask their own governments difficult questions, expose malfeasance, and demand reform. This empowerment is typified by the case of Guyana. Having obtained copies of the newly completed CFAA for Guyana, the opposition, the CSOs, and the media united to disseminate stories about its findings on a regular basis. The stories described the linkages among inadequate PFM practices, the inefficient allocation of scarce public resources, and the reluctance of the private sector to invest. Ultimately, the government decided to proceed with many of the CFAA recommendations (see box 4.1).

**Box 4.1**

## Guyana: The Role of Civil Society and the Media in Promoting Reform

The 2002 CFAA for Guyana found some very substantial weaknesses in the government's PFM systems and practices. Responsibilities for the budget were fragmented. Its systems for compiling the budget as well as its cash and revenue management systems were rudimentary. The revenue management function depended heavily on discretionary application of the rules. The government relied on a manual accounting system, and earlier efforts to automate had been unsuccessful. Furthermore, the internal control and internal audit functions were weak, and there were insufficient numbers of qualified staff. Finally, although the Auditor General's Office was competent and effective, actions were not taken on its audit findings.

The government, however, disagreed with the substance of the CFAA report and initially took no action to implement its findings. But copies of the report were obtained by the opposition and the press. Once the CFAA findings were widely disseminated, they became an important political story, encouraging the government to look again at the recommendations of the report.

Despite its early resistance, the government has made progress in implementing an action plan. It has developed and introduced an integrated financial management system, and many members of the government's accounting and administrative staff have been trained in its use. The new system has already led to better cash and debt management, although because 2007 was the first full year of implementation, a fuller evaluation was possible only beginning in 2008.

- *Broader participation in the global economy.* The Uruguay Round (1986–1994) of the GATT trade talks brought about the biggest reform in the world's trading system since GATT was created at the end of the World War II. The round established new global trading rules, which represented significant steps toward free trade, and led eventually to the establishment of the World Trade Organization. After the Uruguay Round, global trade flows increased (as a percentage of GNP) from 35 percent to 49 percent between 1986 and 2000 and opened up significant opportunities for developing countries (World Bank Indicators Database). But to participate more fully in the global economy, countries had to undertake reforms sufficient to meet the entry requirements for participation and to make them more competitive.

Chile is an example of such a country. In the early 1990s, it returned to civilian rule after nearly 20 years. Its government then embarked on a reform program aimed at making Chile competitive with the United States and the European Union for commerce and at facilitating the raising of funds in international capital markets.

The results from this wave of reforms have been encouraging, led mostly by Brazil and Chile:

- Brazil passed a fiscal responsibility law;
- Chile introduced CHILECOMPRA, the most advanced e-procurement system in the region today;
- Colombia created a high-level steering committee in 2006 to coordinate a procurement reform process, enacted important reforms to the existing law in 2007, and made good progress in e-procurement;
- Honduras enacted a new procurement law in 2001 and revised regulations in 2002, while also introducing new or upgraded financial management systems and addressing the need to upgrade its oversight functions;
- Paraguay developed sound budget and accounting systems that are now being implemented throughout the central administration, and it is in the process of upgrading its oversight arrangements;
- The Dominican Republic upgraded its financial management systems and enacted its first procurement law in 2006;
- Costa Rica reported progress in advancing e-procurement;
- Panama enacted a new procurement law and the corresponding regulations, began developing electronic procurement, and created a central agency responsible for overseeing procurement, developing implementation tools, and settling precontractual complaints.

Despite these efforts, progress has been uneven, as shown in the country-by-country summary tables throughout this book. Progress has also been slow as evidenced by, for example, movement between one CPAR and the subsequent update.[2] Of the seven countries that had CPARs in place prior to the ones used as the basis of this book, only Paraguay made substantial progress in implementing the recommended reforms between the two assessments.

## Remaining Challenges

Significant challenges therefore remain. In particular, the LAC countries continue to have a limited appreciation of the role that independent oversight—exercised by CSOs, SAIs, legislatures, and others—can play in supporting fiscal legitimacy, and such a widespread weakness in oversight continues to undermine the perceived quality of fiscal policy (OECD 2007). Although continuing reforms will take a different path in each country, the following sections set out the priority themes or areas of focus for the LAC countries reviewed, based on the findings in this book.

## Managing for Results

An underlying theme that has emerged is the need for widespread improvements in the management culture. In the LAC region, procurement arrangements developed with a strong control approach and a limited focus on efficiency or value for money. These arrangements evolved in relative isolation from the rest of public administration and not in anticipation of the needs of each country. Furthermore, with some exceptions, procurement reforms have occurred rather hastily when crises exposed deficiencies in systems, and such reforms have typically focused on the technological aspects. Absent has been a holistic approach that recognizes that sustained reform requires an emphasis on achieving specific results aligned with a country's strategic objectives. Possibly the biggest single factor in Chile's improved public sector performance is its recognition that reform starts by shifting management's focus away from inputs toward outputs, outcomes, and impacts. Other LAC countries would benefit from following Chile's example in this respect.

## Legislative Framework for Procurement

The prevailing institutional model in the region is one of central regulation with decentralized implementation of procurement. Although this model could, in theory, provide adaptability to specific agencies' needs, in practice it has promoted a plethora of detailed regulations and processes that generate substantial legal risks and transaction costs for the private sector. Combined with excessive and formalistic regulation, this approach translates into less competition, higher prices, or both. The present international trend to mitigate these problems is to move toward standardization of regulation and instruments while providing the necessary adaptability to specific needs. The LAC countries could benefit from a move in this direction as well. Standardization also contributes to the ability to professionalize, automate, and benchmark these functions and to make it easier to move financial and procurement management staff around government to speed the adoption of more robust practices.

### Internal Controls and Internal Audit

In the area of internal controls what is needed is a change in culture to understand that effective control frameworks, particularly "tone at the top," are critical to laying a foundation for achieving quality in spending. The area of internal audits would benefit from a shift in culture. Instead of viewing the function as a policing one, governments should view it as a consulting activity designed to add value and improve operational effectiveness and efficiency. A starting point for reform programs in this area is to enhance the independence, human resource capacity, and budgets of internal audit units.

### Procurement Staffing

Upgrading the present skills and creating a cadre of qualified procurement and logistics specialists should be high on any reform agenda. Countries should develop and implement professional education and certification programs for procurement specialists, together with an appropriate civil service career path that enables competitive selection and merit-based promotion of skilled personnel. The program should include upgrading of skills and continuing education for the incumbents and identification or creation of professional training and educational programs. As mentioned earlier, standardizing procedures across government units can contribute to professionalizing this function.

### Budget Execution Reporting

Improvements in the quality of spending will not be possible without real-time data on how programs are performing. All countries have invested to some extent in new accounting and budget execution monitoring systems, but some urgently need to modernize, others need to complete the job, and others need to find ways to ensure that information from subnational administrations, typically at the forefront of basic service delivery, is captured. Particular areas in need of a stronger effort are integrating subnational systems with national systems, integrating procurement functions into financial management systems, and promoting the further development and expansion of unified e-procurement systems.

Going forward, a lesson from the past is important: "big-bang" approaches are not always appropriate. At best, they are not cost-effective; at worst, they undermine the government's efforts to build financial and administrative capacity. Initial approaches should therefore concentrate on changing the underlying culture (e.g., imbuing an understanding of the usefulness of regular and timely reporting to the achievement of results) and improving the reporting capabilities of existing systems.

### External Audit

In the area of external audit, the path forward is more stratified. With the good performers, the challenge is to better balance the work program between financial audits and program evaluation. This improvement will require, as a first step, developing enhanced risk assessment frameworks and greater use of computer-assisted audit technologies to better place attention only on those areas that are critical, freeing up resources to tackle issues of operational effectiveness. With the middle performers, the challenge is to move away from ex ante reviews of transactions to ex post audits. A precondition for this step is a strong control framework, including an effective internal audit function. As for the third group of countries, the central issue is to move to a situation in which the SAI is legally independent not just in theory but also in practice. This shift will include actions to ensure that SAIs have the resources they need and do not undertake tasks that are a function of the executive.

Finally, the ROSC A&A reviews reveal that all three groups of countries need to address the professionalization of SAI staffing. In countries in which the SAI is staffed by qualified auditors, professional regulatory frameworks should be strengthened to establish robust licensing criteria as well as to enable rigorous monitoring of compliance with continuing professional education standards. In other countries—more the norm—in which nonspecialist civil servants staff the SAI, consideration should be given to establishing specialized institutions that can provide civil servants with the skills they need to discharge their roles in a public audit function.

### Legislative Oversight

A starting point in strengthening legislative oversight is for countries to develop nonpartisan, technical secretariats to advise legislators on the implications of bills under discussion and on findings in the SAI's annual report. In parallel, countries should make serious efforts to provide easily understood information on spending plans that can be disseminated to enable broader participation in legislative discussions by civil society.

### Civil Society Participation

Ordinary citizens who suffer from the drawbacks and pay the price of poor service delivery are the ones with the greatest interest in demanding good outcomes and accountability for quality performance. In most countries, however, the CSOs that represent the citizenry do not have the tools, skills, or right to information that would enable them to demand accountability. In particular, the level of knowledge about basic procurement is generally low, so stakeholders are at a disadvantage when it comes to public discussions on the topic. A necessary condition for participation is that the relevant information be readily available in accessible forms.

International development institutions have given uneven attention to the importance of CSO oversight and the role of such organizations in promoting reform. Both governments and their international development partners would benefit from learning how to engage constructively with CSOs. The role of CSOs could be enhanced by encouraging well-established CSOs to set up training programs for less capable CSOs. Governments, too, can show their commitment to transparency and accountability by establishing programs to work with CSOs on the design of user-friendly reports and on training to monitor public procurement. Equally important is the establishment of two-way communications through which CSOs can express their concerns and governments can report on actions taken in response to social audit findings (Center on Budget and Policy Priorities 2008).

## Going Forward

In deciding on the direction, extent, and scope of future reforms, the LAC countries and their advisers may wish to take into account several important lessons from PFM and procurement reform programs worldwide:

- *Country-owned vision.* With the exception of Chile, Panama, and to some extent Paraguay, reforms have concentrated almost exclusively on automating systems and introducing or amending laws and the regulatory framework. Although these core elements may be necessary for reform, they must be accompanied by fundamental changes in practices and behavior. Reforms therefore need to address some internalized strategic objectives such as improving sovereign credit ratings, increasing trade competitiveness, stimulating foreign direct investment, or achieving regional geopolitical leadership. Larger strategic objectives could also create incentives for political and managerial leadership for what otherwise might be seen as minor administrative reforms. Chile's PFM reform program exemplifies this point. The program was driven entirely by the government, based on its own analysis of its needs and with an overarching strategic goal of increasing the country's economic competitiveness internationally and its attractiveness to foreign investors. Even though outsiders were asked for technical assistance and financing to support discrete reform elements, there was no question about ownership of the reform process or its purpose.

- *Sustained leadership.* The reform processes in Chile, Guyana, and Honduras enjoyed strong political support, although that support developed differently in each country. In Chile, the executive and legislative leadership agreed to the reform process to achieve legitimacy with the country's citizenry and trading partners. As the benefits of reform quickly became apparent, political support for playing by the rules intensified. Initially, the government of Guyana was unenthusiastic about PFM reform. But once the country's PFM issues were widely covered by the press, the leadership decided to undertake a reform program in order to gain legitimacy with its citizens. Honduras's PFM reforms were driven by the country's leadership, who pushed for a comprehensive action plan. Despite the civil service's strong resistance to many aspects of the program, the political leadership remained resolute in its support for the reforms.

- *Consensus and inclusivity.* The need to create consensus and to obtain public and political support for reform seems obvious, but is often neglected. Interest groups and stakeholders that are not part of the consultative process influence legislators and the media to torpedo or capture reforms. Identifying key players and bringing them to the table, as well as preparing public campaigns that explain in plain language the objectives and the potential benefits, are a critical success factor. All branches of government also need to be on board. Where these conditions are not met, failure is most often the result. For example, recently in the LAC region the executives of two countries were each working in isolation on a new procurement law while a competing draft was being circulated by the legislature in one country and by the Office of the Comptroller General in the other. These competing drafts became difficult to reconcile. The reform efforts collapsed in one case and stalled in the other.

- *Sequence and timing.* Reforms require adequate time for preparation of a credible shared diagnostic, a clear definition of the objectives of reform, the creation of consensus, detailed planning, and finally implementation. The entire sequence may take several years. Chile's successful reform program has now spanned decades and several governments (see box 4.2). Experience also shows that the chances of seeing a reform through are better if the process starts as early as possible in a new administration. Inherited reform programs are likely to be subject, at best, to considerable delays while a new administration gets up to

**Box 4.2**

# Chile: A Comprehensive and Sequenced Reform Program

Chile's PFM reforms grew out of a strong consensus among the government, the opposition, and the legislature to develop and maintain fiscal discipline in the allocation of resources and the expenditure of public funds. This consensus was driven by a broadly shared desire to become trading partners with and obtain investment financing from the United States and the European Union. As a result, Chile has PFM arrangements that are best practice in the region and come close to achieving internationally recognized standards.

Chile's broad program of public sector reforms began in the early 1990s, when Chile was one of the first countries in the region to use computerized systems for budgeting and accounting. Although the two systems were related and used the same expenditure classifications, they were not integrated; information was exchanged between them using computer tapes and other manual interventions. In the mid-1990s, these systems were considered good by regional standards, so the government did not seek to upgrade them. Instead, it sought to ensure that the PFM functions were staffed by an adequate number of qualified professionals and that public sector managers were trained in the use of modern management techniques.

Enhanced transparency was also an important component of this first wave of reforms. The government developed an extensive reporting framework and facilitated the wide dissemination of its reports. Chile was thus one of the region's first countries to routinely post budget information on the Web. Even in areas in which the government has felt justified in not providing complete information to the public, it has made efforts to be relatively transparent. For example, although the government excludes the Ministry of Defense and the national copper company from its detailed budget and accounting systems, it requires both of those organizations to provide summary reports to the public on a regular basis, and it includes summary figures for both organizations in the budget and the consolidated accounts.

These reforms also placed significant emphasis on developing and maintaining an effective control environment and an internal audit function staffed with adequate numbers of qualified personnel. The result is that with a strong internal control framework in place, the SAI is able to focus attention on program evaluation and value for money audits.

The sustained reforms in Chile have become the basis for ongoing improvements, including the adoption of accrual accounting. A management culture of respect for rules permeates the government, PFM functions are professionally staffed at all levels, public sector managers expect good information and use it for decision making, and transparency is scrupulously observed at all levels of government.

speed and, at worst, to cancellation if not consistent with the new administration's priorities. Finally, it is important in the initial stages to focus on introducing changes that can produce immediate, measurable improvements to encourage sustained commitment by all involved in the process.

- *Basics first.* Chile's experience demonstrates that while an integrated financial management information system is today a prerequisite, it need not be state-of-the-art in order for a country to undertake broader or deeper reforms. In fact, an antiquated system that is well understood and provides adequate information to staff and managers may be more beneficial than a state-of-the-art system that is poorly understood or provides only marginal benefits. At least as important as the hardware is the basic need to develop a stable cadre of suitably qualified financial and administrative staff. A maxim therefore to keep in mind: "Reformers should focus on the basics on which reform is built, not on particular techniques . . . and should build institutional mechanisms that support and demand a performance orientation for all dimensions" (Schick 1998).

The LAC countries have undertaken extensive debates about the most effective structures for the internal audit functions, the appropriate balance of power between the executive and the legislature, just how much of a "right to know" should be granted the media, and the role of SAIs. These questions will have to be settled for sustained progress in PFM and procurement reforms that can lead to a permanent improvement in the quality of public spending. Even if not driven by a domestic agenda of openness and better governance, sustained progress in reforms is needed for the region to participate more broadly and competitively in the global economy. Particularly because of the current global economic crises, LAC countries have little choice but to adopt or adapt internationally recognized benchmarks already established for the management of public finances. The sooner progress is made, the less countries will be driven by crises to enact the patchwork of poorly informed reforms of the past, with the result that LAC governments will be come to be seen as better stewards of the public trust.

## Notes

1. In April 2008 in Paraguay, the victory of presidential candidate Fernando Lugo ended a 61-year period of unbroken rule by the Colorado Party. Lugo

campaigned on a platform of addressing the backlog of needed structural reforms. The new administration thus issued the Paraguay Economic and Social Plan 2008–2013, which addresses, among other things, improvements in public sector management and governance.

2. Updates are typically undertaken at five-year intervals.

# Bibliography

Center on Budget and Policy Priorities. 2008. "Our Money, Our Responsibility." International Budget Partnership. http://www.internationalbudget.org.

Corporación Latinobarómetro. 2008. *Latinobarometro Report*. Santiago: Corporación Latinobarómetro.

Deloitte. 2007. "IFRSs in Your Pocket 2007: An IAS Plus Guide." Deloitte Touche Tohmatsu LLP. http://www.iasplus.com/dttpubs/pocket2008.pdf.

ECLAC (Economic Commission for Latin America and the Caribbean). 2008. *Foreign Investment in Latin America and the Caribbean 2007*. Santiago: United Nations.

EIU Country Data: World Commodity Forecasts Database. *The Economist*, Economist Intelligence Unit.

FASB (Financial Accounting Standards Board). 2007. "Facts about FASB." http://72.3.243.42/facts/tech_agenda.shtml.

IASB (International Accounting Standards Board). 2007. "IASB and the IASC Foundation. Who We Are and What We Do." http://www.iasb.org/NR/rdonlyres/95C54002-7796-4E23-A327-28D23D2F55EA/0/WhoWeAre_Revise5Feb09.pdf.

IFAC (International Federation of Accountants). 2007a. "Identifying and Assessing the Risks of Material Misstatement Through Understanding the Entity and Its Environment." International Standard on Auditing 315.

———. 2007b. "International Public Sector Accounting Standards Board Factsheet." http://www.ifac.org/PublicSector/.

———. 2007c. "IPSAS Adoption by Governments." http://www.ifac.org/PublicSector/Downloads/IPSAS_Adoption_Governments.pdf.

IIARF (Institute of Internal Auditors Research Foundation). 2004. *The Professional Practices Framework.* Altamonte Springs, FL: IIARF, January.

IIF (Institute of International Finance). 2009. "2009 to See Sharp Declines in Capital Flows to Emerging Markets, Says IIF." Press release, January 27. IIE, Washington, DC.

IMF (International Monetary Fund). 2001. "Government Finance Statistics Manual 2001." http://www.imf.org/external/pubs/ft/gfs/manual/.

INTOSAI (International Organization of Supreme Audit Institutions). http://www.intosai.org/en/portal/.

———. 1977. "The Lima Declaration of Guidelines on Auditing Precepts." Brussels, October.

———. 2004. *Guidelines for Internal Control Standards for the Public Sector.* Brussels: INTOSAI.

Moody's Investors Services. 2008. *Moody's Statistical Handbook: Country Credit.* May. http://www.moodys.com/moodys/cust/content/content.ashx?source=StaticContent/BusinessLines/Sovereign-SubSovereign/CountryCredit.pdf.

National Association of State Boards of Accountancy. http://www.nasba.org/nasbaweb/NASBAWeb.nsf/WPHP?OpenForm.

Nef, Jorge. 2003. "The Culture of Distrust in Latin American Public Administration." International Association of Schools and Institutes of Administration. Paper presented at the Conference on Public Administration, Challenges of Inequality and Exclusion, September 14–18, Miami, FL.

Nielse, Ruth, and Steen Treumer. 2005. *The New EU Procurement Directives.* Copenhagen: Djof Publishing.

Ocampo, Jose Antonio. 2003. "Latin America's Growth Frustrations: The Macro and Mesoeconomic Links." Paper delivered at the Seminar on Management of Volatility, Financial Liberalization and Growth in Emerging Economies, April 24–25. United Nations Economic Commission for Latin America and the Caribbean, Santiago.

OECD (Organisation for Economic Co-operation and Development). 2003. "Budgeting in Brazil." *OECD Journal on Budgeting* 3 (1).

———. 2005. *Economic Survey of Brazil, 2005: Strengthening Social Policies and Expenditure.* OECD Economics Department. Paris: OECD.

———. 2006. *Methodology for Assessment of National Procurement Systems.* OECD Development Assistance Committee (later renamed Development Co-operation Directorate). Paris: OECD.

———. 2007. *Latin American Economic Outlook 2008*. OECD Development Centre. Paris: OECD.

Pastor, Manuel, Jr. 1990. *Capital Flight and the Latin American Debt Crisis*. Washington, DC: Economic Policy Institute.

Pendle, George. 1990. *A History of Latin America*. Harmondsworth, U.K.: Pan Books.

Santiso, Carlos. 2004. "Legislatures and Budget Oversight in Latin America: Strengthening Public Finance Accountability in Emerging Economies." *OECD Journal on Budgeting* 4 (2).

Schick, Allen. 1998. *A Contemporary Approach to Public Expenditure Management*. Washington, DC: World Bank Institute.

Trepte, Peter. 2004. *Regulating Procurement*. New York: Oxford University Press.

U.K. Department for International Development. 2004. "Characteristics of Different External Audit Models." Policy Division Information Series Briefing, Ref. no. PD Info 021. London.

UNCITRAL (United Nations Commission on International Trade Law). 1999. *Model Law on Procurement of Goods, Construction and Services, with Guide to Enactment*. New York: United Nations.

World Bank. 1998. *Public Expenditure Management Handbook*. Washington, DC: World Bank, June.

———. 2001a. *Colombia: Country Procurement Assessment Report*. Report no. 32011-CO. Washington, DC: World Bank, March 1.

———. 2001b. *Peru: Country Financial Accountability Assessment Report*. Report no. 25729. Washington, DC: World Bank, February.

———. 2002a. *Brazil: Country Financial Accountability Assessment*. Report no. 25685-BR. Washington, DC: World Bank, June 30.

———. 2002b. *Guyana: Country Financial Accountability Assessment*. Report no. 24289-GY. Washington, DC: World Bank, June 6.

———. 2003. *Mexico: Country Financial Accountability Assessment Report*. Report no. 29155-MX. Washington, DC: World Bank, September 5.

———. 2004a. *Brazil: Country Procurement Assessment Report*. Report no. 29766-BR. Washington, DC: World Bank, March 1.

———. 2004b. *Chile: Country Procurement Assessment Report*. Report no. 28914-CL. Washington, DC: World Bank, August 1.

———. 2004c. *Honduras: Country Financial Accountability Assessment*. Report no. 28418-HO. Washington, DC: World Bank, January 3.

———. 2004d. *Paraguay: Country Financial Accountability Assessment*. Report no. 30084-PY. Washington, DC: World Bank, August 26.

——. 2005a. *Chile: Country Financial Accountability Assessment.* Report no. 32630-CL. Washington, DC: World Bank, June 27.

——. 2005b. *Colombia: Country Financial Accountability Assessment.* Report no. 31915-CO. Washington, DC: World Bank, April 13.

——. 2005c. *Costa Rica: Country Financial Accountability Assessment.* Report no. 34976-CR. Washington, DC: World Bank, June 30.

——. 2005d. *Dominican Republic: Country Fiduciary Assessment.* Report no. 31497-DR. Washington, DC: World Bank, April 18.

——. 2005e. *Guatemala: Country Financial Accountability and Procurement Assessment Report.* Report no. 35040-GT. Washington, DC: World Bank, June 24.

——. 2005f. *Honduras: Country Procurement Assessment Report.* Report no. 32791-HO. Washington, DC: World Bank, February 1.

——. 2005g. *Peru: Country Procurement Assessment Report Update.* Report no. 35068-PE. Washington, DC: World Bank, November.

——. 2006a. *Costa Rica: Country Procurement Assessment Report.* Report no. 39594-CR. Washington, DC: World Bank, November.

——. 2006b. *El Salvador: Report on the Observance of Standards and Codes (ROSC): Accounting and Auditing.* Washington, DC: World Bank, October.

——. 2006c. *Honduras: Public Financial Management Report.* Washington, DC: World Bank, June.

——. 2006d. *Jamaica: Joint Country Financial Accountability Assessment and Country Procurement Assessment.* Report no. 34962-JM. Washington, DC: World Bank, April 12.

——. 2006e. *Panama: Country Financial Accountability and Procurement Assessment Report.* Report no. 40496-PA. Washington, DC: World Bank, December 31.

——. 2006f. *Paraguay: Public Expenditure Review.* Report no. 32797-PY. Washington, DC: World Bank.

——. 2007. *Mexico: The Federal Procurement System: Challenges and Opportunities.* Report no. 47401. Washington, DC: World Bank, November 1.

——. 2008a. *Argentina: Country Financial Accountability Assessment Report.* Report no. 39228-AR. Washington, DC: World Bank, March

——. 2008b. *Paraguay: Integrated Fiduciary Assessment.* Report no. 44007-PY. Washington, DC: World Bank.

——. 2008c. *Social Safety Nets in Peru, 2008 Report.* Washington, DC: World Bank.

——. 2008d. *World Development Indicators Report 2008.* Washington, DC: World Bank.

World Development Indicators Database. World Bank, Washington, DC.

# Index

*Boxes, notes, and tables are indicated by b, n, and t, respectively.*

## A

accountability and transparency
  demand for, 3, 80, 81b
  excessive procedural formalities
    affecting, 61–62
accounting
  global developments in, 24–27
  LAC practices, 6, 27–30, 51–52n21
*Acuerdo Gubernativo*, Guatemala,
    21n14, 77n9
ADR (alternative dispute resolution), 61,
    69, 77n6
aggregate fiscal discipline, 10, 23–24,
    30–33, 33t
alternative dispute resolution (ADR), 61,
    69, 77n6
American Institute of Internal Auditors,
    43–44
arbitration, 61, 69, 77n6
Argentina
  additional report data from, 5
  budget comprehensiveness in, 31, 32
  budget execution reporting in, 13
  IPSAS standards, 29
  regulation of procurement procedures
    in, 10, 60

ROSC A&A review of, 50n5
stimulus package in, 20n6
audit
  external. *See* external audit
  global developments in, 24–27
  internal control and audit framework,
    13–14, 42–44, 48t, 49, 84
  in LAC, 6, 27–30
  Lima Declaration of Guidelines on
    Auditing Precepts, 26, 45–47
  risk- and performance-based, 14
  SAIs. *See* supreme audit institutions
Australia, 29
automated information systems, 9

## B

Baker Plan, 80
Barbados, 29
Bolivia, 1
Brady Bonds, 24, 50n2, 80
Brady, Nicholas, 8
Brazil
  accounting system in, 51–52n21
  aggregate fiscal discipline in, 10, 30, 31,
    32, 33t
  automated information systems in, 9

# P

Sarbanes-Oxley Act of 2002 (U.S.), 5
sequencing and timing of reform,
    87–89, 88*b*
Sopher, Jamil, xiv
South Africa, 51*n*12
sovereign debt. *See* debt and debt relief
St. Vincent and the Grenadines, 7, 29
staffing. *See* human resources
stimulus packages, 2, 20*n*6
strategic resource allocation, 23–24,
    33–37, 37*t*
student performance, PISA measurement
    of, 50, 52*n*25
subnational budget reporting, 12–13, 31
subnational procurement regulation, 60
supreme audit institutions (SAIs)
    areas of progress and remaining
        challenges for external audit,
        14–15
    CSO participation and oversight, 16*b*
    independence of, 45–46
    INTOSAI, 26, 45
    legislative oversight and, 17
    Lima Declaration of Guidelines on
        Auditing Precepts, 26, 45–47
    procurement, independent oversight of,
        71–72
    reform challenges, 85
    role in external audit process, 45–47, 49,
        52*n*23
system management of procurement
    process, 65*b*

**T**

Tarallo, Roberto, x
TI (Transparency International), 5, 80
timing and sequencing of reform,
    87–89, 88*b*
trade associations influencing procurement
    practices in LAC, 57–58
trade liberalization. *See* free trade
transparency and accountability
    demand for, 3, 80, 81*b*
    excessive procedural formalities
        affecting, 61–62

Transparency International (TI), 5, 80
Trinidad and Tobago, 1

**U**

UNCITRAL (United Nations Commission
    on International Trade Law), 55
UNDP (United Nations Development
    Programme), 62, 63*b*
United Kingdom (U.K.), 5, 27, 29, 50*n*7
United Nations Commission on
    International Trade Law
    (UNCITRAL), 55
United Nations Convention on the
    Recognition and Enforcement of
    Foreign Arbitral Awards, 69
United Nations Development Programme
    (UNDP), 62, 63*b*
United Nations Office for Project
    Services, 62
United States
    accounting, auditing, and reporting
        developments with global effects,
        24–26
    Chilean credibility as trading partner
        for, 39
    economic stimulus package in, 2
    GAAP, 25, 28, 29
    global benchmarks in public financial
        management and procurement
        from, 5
    IPSAS standards in, 29
    legal heritage of LAC, influence on,
        27–28
Uruguay, 29, 50*n*5
Uruguay Round, GATT, 55, 81

**V**

vision, role of, 64–65, 86

**W**

Westminster Model, 27, 50*n*7
World Bank, x, xvii–xix, 27, 76*n*2, 80
World Trade Organization (WTO),
    5, 55, 81

www.ingramcontent.com/pod-product-compliance
Lightning Source LLC
Chambersburg PA
CBHW070926270326
41927CB00011B/2743